BEST F
GREA

Scott Marchant

50 Hikes within Two Hours of Boise

Published by Hiking Idaho
P.O. Box 9498
Boise, ID 83707

ISBN 978-0-9977370-7-3

Cover photo: Ten Mile Creek, hike 27
Title Page photo: Halverson Lakes, hike 44
Photography by Scott Marchant
Edited by Cristen Iris
Book design by Kiran Spees
Printed in the United States

Liability Waiver

Due to the possibility of personal error, typographical error, misinterpretation, and the many changes both natural and man-made, *Best Easy Hikes Greater Boise*, its author, publisher, and all other persons or companies directly and indirectly associated with this publication assume no responsibility for accidents, injury, death, damage or any losses by individuals or groups using this publication.

Outdoor activities are always potentially dangerous. Good decision-making skills and astute judgment will help reduce potential hazards and risks. Prepare yourself with proper equipment and outdoor skills, and you will have an enjoyable experience.

Every effort has been made by the author to ensure the accuracy of the information in this guide. However, things often change once a guide is published—areas fall under new management, trails are rerouted, private land is acquired by the public, trailhead signs are destroyed or modified, wildfires impact areas, etc. Corrections, updates and suggestions may be sent to the author at scott@hikingidaho.com.

Preface

"That I am a saner, healthier, more contented man, with truer standards of life, for all my loiterings in the fields and woods, I am fully convinced."
—John Burroughs from *The Gospel of Nature*

Welcome to *Best Easy Hikes Greater Boise*. The inspiration for this guidebook was initially conceived back in the summer of 2013. I will never forget an enthusiastic gentleman who approached me at my booth at the Capital City Public Market in Boise and said how much he enjoyed getting into the beauty of nature but found it difficult to tackle hikes that are steep or long. The idea of trekking 7 or 8 miles over a 10,000-foot pass sounded about as appealing as a root canal. Over the next several years, many more hikers, young and old and everything in between, echoed similar thoughts. I finally realized there was a need for a guidebook with quality hike experiences that are not too physically challenging.

Two years ago, I started researching hiking trails with a new goal—to identify trails that are both scenic and manageable for most individuals. Whether the hiker was short on time or in need of a simple outing, the hikes needed to fit the desires of families, novice hikers and include routes that introduced the seasoned veteran to unfamiliar trails. It did not mean that the hikes were necessarily urban or a twenty-minute drive from home. In fact, some of the trails in this guidebook see fewer people in a year than some of the Boise foothill hikes see in a week. My desire was to expose individuals to a broad collection of "easy" hikes in which the experience and scenery is often as rewarding as those that require a lengthy hike into the wilderness.

One of my new insights while researching the guidebook was that you do not have to immerse yourself in the woods for great lengths of time to obtain the restorative powers of nature. Whether you walk a half-mile or ten, stay for an hour or overnight or drive five minutes or two hours to a trailhead, the most important aspect is just putting your feet on the ground and opening your senses to the natural world around you. Mother Nature's doors are always open, and her classroom is rarely full. Take the time to pay her a visit, and your body, mind and soul will thank you. I hope you enjoy where this book takes you.

Scott Marchant

Trail Locations

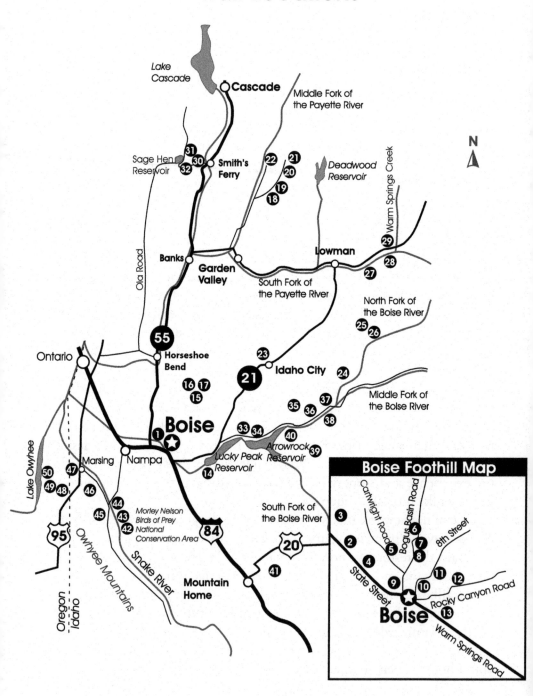

Contents

Introduction

The brutally honest and passionate nature writer Edward Abbey wrote: "Beyond the wall of the unreal city there is another world waiting for you. It is the old true world of the deserts, the mountains, the forests." Anyone who knows the rugged landscape of southwest Idaho knows Treasure Valley is truly blessed with this old world. The high desert near the Owyhee Mountains, the convoluted hills and gulches of the Boise foothills, the old-growth forests and mountains in the recesses of the Boise National Forest and the rugged, complex canyons along the Middle Fork of the Boise River all beckon to be explored.

Best Easy Hikes Greater Boise explores a network of fifty trails within two hours of Boise. A little less than a third of the book is dedicated to the Boise Front with the remaining trails located in or near Leslie Gulch, the Owyhee foothills, the Snake River Canyon, the Middle Fork of the Boise River, Sage Hen Reservoir and the forests near Idaho City, Lowman and Garden Valley. The diversity of the hikes is remarkable: from well-trod trails near Boise to lonely and little-known paths further away. The one common theme—all the hikes are doable without a huge investment of time or physical effort.

So, what exactly is an easy hike? For the purpose of this book, an easy hike is defined as an outing to a defined destination that requires a hike of less than 5 miles (out-and-back or as a loop) and with less than 1,000 feet of gain. Even within the confines of this definition, you will find a great deal of variety. The shortest hike in the book is about a half-mile with little elevation gain—perfect for families with young children or those short on time. At the other end of the spectrum are longer "easy" hikes near 5 miles with enough elevation gain to require a little perspiration. Even on the longer hikes, there are suggestions for mini-destinations allowing the hike to be shortened. Most of the hikes are in the 2- to 4-mile range.

With most hiking books, it is easy to identify a journey's end because it is often a mountain lake or high peak. The very nature of a short, easy hike precludes many of these destinations since you would have to hike a lengthy distance or ascend a long and steep grade. The author paid keen attention to possible destinations including meadows, outcroppings, creek-side settings and ridges with exceptional views. If you complete every hike in this guidebook, you will experience a surprising assortment of Idaho's scenery: hot springs, flower-covered hillsides, tumbling waterfalls, crystal-clear creeks, wild river corridors, rugged canyons, alpine meadows and wind-swept ridges. You will also have outstanding opportunities to see birds, animals and a wide range of flora.

All the information in this book was compiled by the author over the last two years. Each trail was hiked at least once but most of them multiple times. One of the great rewards of hiking all the routes is the opportunity to learn the terrain intimately—what makes one canyon or creek different from another and how they may be similar. The descriptions of topography, flora and fauna are all based on experience.

USING THIS GUIDE

If this is your first time using this type of a guidebook, here is a brief introduction regarding how to find a hike that fits your needs. In the front of the book, there is a Location Map. Seek out the hikes in the area you wish to visit or are already near. Next, review the at-a-glance information at the top of each hike. Consider mileage, difficulty and total elevation gain. Once you have narrowed your search to a few hikes, read the brief description (under the at-a-glance information) to get a better idea of the hike you are considering.

Each hike has four primary sections:
- Twelve, key at-a-glance details (described below).

- A general description of the hike. Think of this as the sizzle—why you would want to hike this trail. Details include fauna, flora, historical references, scenery, backpacking opportunities and alternate hiking options. The description gives you a good impression of what it feels like to hike the trail. You will also find (if there are opportunities) suggestions for dispersed camping at primitive sites or campgrounds.

- Detailed trailhead directions.

- A comprehensive description of the hike. This includes detailed information concerning mileage, unsigned and signed junctions, creek and river fords, off-trail options, specific information regarding backpack campsites, possible destinations to shorten or lengthen the hike and information about flora and fauna. Cumulative distances are given, so you can tailor any hike to fit your time constraints and physical abilities.

At-a-glance details include:

- **Distance** – All distances were measured using a GPS and are reported to the closest one-tenth of a mile. Out-and-back distances were measured from the trailhead to the hike's final destination, then back to the trailhead.

- **Total Elevation Gain** – This is how much climbing you will be doing during the hike. The total elevation gain is the cumulative amount of ascending required from the trailhead to the final destination and then back to the trailhead. To compute the total elevation gain, the elevation gain is added to the elevation loss. For example, on an out-and-back hike, if you ascend 200 feet to a ridge and descend 100 feet to a creek, your total gain for the hike is 300 feet. This is because on your return, you will need to hike back up the 100 feet you descended.

- **Difficulty** – Each trip is rated for its difficulty. The rating is based on an individual in good physical condition. There is some subjectivity in the ratings with consideration given to trail conditions, route-finding, creek fords, etc. The three possible ratings are:

  🚶 – You might think of this as a stroll in the park. There will be very few hills to climb and a total elevation gain of less than 300 feet. Hiking distances are between 1 and 2 miles out-and-back.

  🚶🚶 – The hiking distances are longer at 2 to 3 miles. There will be a few more hills to climb, although elevation gains will be less than 500 feet.

  🚶🚶🚶 – These are the most demanding easy hikes and will have elevation gains of more than 500 feet. There will likely be steep grades. Distances range from 3 to 5 miles. A few of the hikes, those with gains of more than 700 feet, might be considered moderate by some hikers.

- **Elevation Range** – These figures represent the trail's highest and lowest points, not necessarily the beginning and ending elevations. Normally, the lowest elevation will be the trailhead. Elevations are given in feet and rounded to within the nearest 50 feet. For example, if a hike ends at a 3,489-foot ridge, it is listed as 3,500 feet. Elevation range information is valuable when you are hiking in late fall, winter and early spring when you are likely to encounter snow. If you have an idea of the snow elevation levels in an area, you can predict whether you will be able to hike a particular trail.

- **Topographic Map** – This refers to the U. S. Geological Survey (USGS) 1:24,000 maps that correspond to the referenced hike. The maps are the most detailed available and show forest cover, significant creeks, rivers and lakes. They also indicate steepness of terrain. You will find the maps an invaluable resource not only to identify key topographical features but also for navigation purposes if you go off trail. Sections of the USGS 1:24,000 maps are included in the book for each hike. The route is labeled as a heavy black and white broken line. Off-trail routes are labeled as black dots.

- **Time** – It is impossible to accurately predict hiking times because everybody hikes at a different speed. This guidebook uses a conservative 2 mph. The times listed are subjective and based on a hiker in reasonably good health. The time to complete the hike does not include breaks for eating, photography or resting. Many factors such as wet trails, poor visibility, snow, difficult creek or river fords, route-finding, deadfall and poor trail conditions can slow you down.

- **Seasons** – Here you will find the months that the hiking route is normally accessible. Obviously, it is impossible to predict when snow will melt in the high country, when creeks will be low enough to ford or when snow will appear in the fall. No two years are alike, and trails can open sooner or later than listed times. Use your own judgement when planning a hike, and contact the local ranger district office for conditions.

- **Water Availability** – This provides a list of streams, creeks and lakes where you will find water. Most sources are reliable throughout the year. You should purify all water before drinking.

- **Cautionary Advice** – This alerts you to possible hazards on a hike. Trail conditions may change, and new, unknown hazards may emerge.

- **Additional Information** – This is the agency, phone number and/or website that you can contact for more information.

- **Pit Latrine** – This identifies whether a pit toilet is available at the trailhead. In some instances, there may be a pit latrine at a nearby campground.

- **GPS Coordinates** – All GPS coordinates are listed as WGS84 datum. When using a GPS, make sure it is set to navigate with WGS84 datum. The coordinates for trailheads and final destinations are provided in degrees with minutes as decimals.

- **Trail User Symbols** – The symbols above the coordinates header alerts you to the type of users allowed on a route. Trails are often reevaluated and designations can change. On many of the trails, a user class—usually motor bikes—may be restricted to a limited section of the trail.

 Hikers   Mountain Bikes

 Equestrians   Motorized

TRAILHEAD ACCESS, SIGNS AND TRAIL CONDITION

Most of the trailheads in this guide are accessible with a passenger car. If a high-clearance vehicle is recommended, it is noted in the text. Driving distances were calculated with a vehicle tripmeter. Different vehicles will vary slightly in their measurements of distance.

Many of the trails are accessed along dirt roads. Early season hikers traveling in the high country may encounter downed trees, washouts and fallen rock debris before the roads are serviced and repaired. The roads may be impassable, and you should use sound judgement when encountering road hazards.

Although many trailheads and trail junctions are signed, be aware that some are not. Even signs that exist today are often destroyed by weather, fire or vandalism. Some trails, often

A well-marked trailhead

Cairns often mark ill-defined trails

those through burned forest, washouts or areas where trees do not exist, will have rock cairns identifying a route. A cairn is a stack of rocks, usually shaped like a pyramid, that was obviously created by human hands. Cairns are also used to identify unsigned junctions and mountain summits.

The majority of trails in this guidebook are maintained by Ridge to Rivers staff, the U.S. Forest Service and volunteers. A few trails, although clearly defined due to use, are not official trails, and, thus, do not receive any trail maintenance. You may encounter deadfall and confusing paths (often created by game) on these hikes. High-use trails receive annual maintenance while others fall on a rotation system. Hiking Idaho encourages readers to support the Idaho Trails Association, which organizes volunteer trail stewardship projects for the construction and maintenance of Idaho trails. Visit their website at idahotrailsassociation. org for more information.

WILDERNESS CONSERVATION

Pristine and abundant wilderness is one of Idaho's most treasured resources. It cannot be overstated how fragile the environment is at higher elevations. Plants contend with a variety of stresses including cold nights, poor soil, hot days, short growing seasons and sometimes little moisture. On top of these natural challenges, the plant community must contend with the impact from hikers and backpackers. What the wilderness looks like tomorrow will depend on how well the people of today take care of it. We can do many things to protect the land for future generations.
Follow these simple rules when you are in the backcountry:

- If you pack something in, pack it out.

- Minimize campfire impacts. Backcountry stoves are very efficient, and cooking with fire is unnecessary.

- Bury human waste in a 6- to 8-inch hole at least 100 feet from other campsites, trails and water sources. Carry your used toilet paper out in a plastic bag.

Stay off trails when they are muddy

- Do not cut switchbacks. This causes erosion and additional trail maintenance is then required.

- Respect wildlife.

- Be sure to leave all items—plants, rocks, artifacts, animals—as you find them.

- Minimize campsites. When camping in an established campsite, cluster the tents close, and don't expand the compacted area by spreading out. When camping at a pristine site, remove all traces of your stay.

- Hike single-file in the middle of the trail, even when it's wet or muddy, to avoid trampling vegetation.

TRAIL ETIQUETTE

Horses, Mountain Bikers, Motorized Vehicles and Other Hikers

The general rule in the wilderness is that mountain bikers and motorized vehicles yield to hikers, and hikers yield to horses and pack animals. When approached by horses or pack animals, you should get off the trail and sit or stand quietly until the animal has passed. Horseback riders will often let hikers know the habits of their animals.

Bikers are supposed to yield to hikers, but it makes more sense for a hiker to yield. When approached by a bike, especially on a steep hill, it is much easier for a hiker to step aside.

Motorized users should yield to all other users. It is unlikely you will encounter any motorized users, except where noted in the hike description.

Hiking with Dogs

When hiking with pets, they must be under voice control or physical restraint at all times. This includes preventing your dog from pursuing wildlife and barking at other trail users. Carry a leash, and be prepared to use it when necessary. Clean up after your dog the same way you would with human waste: Bury it in a hole that is 6- to 8-inches deep and 100 feet away from all campsites, water and trails.

Several of the trails within the Ridge to Rivers trail network require pets to be on leash at all times. This information is posted at the trailhead. Trails on which pets must be on leash at all times are noted in the cautionary advice.

HIKING SAFETY

Although hiking is relatively safe, the very nature of being outdoors is potentially hazardous. Many people overestimate the possibility of encounters with large animals in the backcountry. In reality, the greatest dangers are from falling, drowning and getting lost. Here are a few tips to help you explore the wilderness safely.

Falls – The good news is you can usually control the situation by deciding whether you want to expose yourself to a potential fall. Be careful and use sound judgement when traversing a ledge or climbing a rock. Remember, it's a lot easier to climb up than down. Trekking poles are very helpful for maintaining your balance in hazardous conditions. Step over rocks, deadfall and roots rather than on them. These surfaces are often very slippery, and it is easy to trip or twist an ankle, especially on slopes.

Creek and River Crossings – Use good judgement when fording creeks and rivers. Don't underestimate the power of moving water, especially during spring runoff. As a rule, don't cross fast-moving water that is more than knee deep. Crossing waterways with water levels above mid-thigh gives the current a large surface area to push against. When hiking with children, be very careful around moving water, and teach children the dangers of high-water levels.

Tips for Safely Fording Creeks and Rivers:
- When approaching a creek or river ford, study the waterway both upstream and downstream. The water will usually be the shallowest where the waterway is widest.
- Walk slowly across the creek, and firmly plant each foot before lifting the other.

- Consider keeping your boots on to help support your ankles and maintain firm footing.

- Before crossing, look for deadfall that may bridge the creek. Remember that trees can be very slippery, especially in early morning when they may be covered with a thin layer of ice.

- If a creek has a sandy bottom, consider fording the creek in a pair of sandals. This will keep your boots dry.

Use deadfall as a bridge.

- Trekking poles can provide additional stability when fording a creek.

- Make sure to place your camera and other items in watertight containers before crossing fast-moving water.

Hypothermia – Anyone who hikes should be aware of hypothermia—what it is and how to prevent it. In simple terms, hypothermia is the lowering of body temperature caused by loss of heat through the skin faster than the body is producing heat. Initial symptoms include shivering and the loss of physical and mental abilities. Severe hypothermia can lead to death.

Temperatures do not have to be below freezing for hypothermia to set in. Most cases occur when outside temperatures are between 30°F and 50°F. Be especially cautious in windy and wet conditions because body heat is wicked away by wind and water.

The good news is, hypothermia is easy to prevent, and clothing is your best defense. Think layers: Wool and synthetic clothing are best. Bring a light windbreaker, waterproof shell, gloves, a hat and wool socks. Cotton is a terrible choice because when it gets wet, it can increase conductive heat loss by a factor of five.

Heatstroke/Heat Exhaustion – At the other extreme, hot weather and strenuous physical activity can cause serious heat-related problems. Heatstroke occurs when body temperature reaches 104°F or higher. Heat exhaustion is a milder heat-related syndrome that may include heavy sweating and a rapid pulse. Left untreated, heat exhaustion can lead to heatstroke, a life-threatening condition.

Fortunately, both heatstroke and heat exhaustion are preventable. Drink plenty of liquids and wear a hat. Avoid exposed trails during the early afternoon, which is usually the hottest part of the day. If someone in your party develops symptoms of heat exhaustion, have the person sit in shade or a cool place and drink plenty of fluids.

Lightning – Storms can build quickly, and hikers should constantly observe weather conditions. If lightning threatens, make it a priority to get below the tree line. Keep out of meadows and away from lone trees or rocks. If you are caught in an exposed location, discard metal objects, and squat on two feet keeping as low to the ground as possible. Stay at least 20 feet away from others in your group so one strike does not incapacitate your entire group.

The Sun – One of the most underrated dangers in the wilderness is the effects of the sun. Prolonged exposure to the sun can cause sunburn, snow blindness, heat exhaustion, heat stroke and dehydration. Extended exposure can cause skin cancer and permanent damage to the skin. Remember, the sun's effects are more pronounced at higher altitudes. Key pieces of gear that every hiker should have include:

• A lightweight, long-sleeve shirt to provide UV protection.

• A wide-brimmed hat to protect ears and face.

• Sunscreen with an SPF rating of at least 15.

• Polarized sunglasses to protect eyes from UV rays.

• Water. Dehydration can easily sneak up on you while hiking. Do not

Entrance to Leslie Gulch

underestimate your water requirements. A good rule of thumb is to carry 2 quarts of water per person. Many packs today include a water carrier. Remember, water is heavy. One gallon weighs more than 8 pounds. A flexible option is to carry a water filter. There are many types of water treatment systems today. Most are relatively inexpensive, lightweight and easy to use.

Blisters – When hiking, your feet should be one of your top priorities. There is nothing like painful blisters to ruin a hiking trip. Avoid blisters by taking these precautions:

- Break in new hiking boots or shoes before you hike.
- Wear lightweight, breathable shoes.
- Wear quality socks that provide both cushion and breathability.
- Carry moleskin, and use it as soon as you feel a hot spot.

Rattlesnakes – Although rattlesnakes are venomous, their menacing reputation is not deserved. Of the approximately 7,500 venomous snake bites each year in the United States, on average, fewer than six people die. You are more likely to be involved in a traffic accident driving to the trailhead than be bitten by a rattlesnake. Regardless, here are a few suggestions. Rattlesnakes are most active when outside temperatures are between 77°F and 89°F. Be especially alert in the late morning and afternoon when you are most likely to find them sunning on a rock.

Rattlers' survival strategy falls in this order: camouflage, escape and defense. If you see a rattlesnake, walk around it, and do not provoke it. If you are bitten, try to remain calm, and get to a medical facility as soon as possible. Remember, most rattlesnakes do not inject a significant amount of venom when they bite.

Your Ego – The vast majority of outdoor mishaps are preventable. Do not overestimate your capability whether fording a creek, traversing an exposed ridge, hiking off-trail or hiking long distances. The wilderness is not the place to make errors in judgement. Remember, a GPS, smartphone or high-tech watch may be the latest technological gadget, but they cannot stop you from drowning or falling and can certainly give you a false sense of security while you're in the backcountry.

Be Prepared – You should always have a first-aid kit and proper clothing. Let someone know where you are going—very important if you are hiking alone—and when you expect to return. Make sure you are in good physical health. Knowledge is your best ally when in the wilderness.

WEATHER

Hikes in this book range from elevations near 2,300 feet along the Snake River to 7,300 feet at Shafer Butte. Due to the 5,000-foot elevation difference, weather conditions and accessibility are varied.

Boise Foothills, Middle Fork of the Boise River, Snake River and Leslie Gulch Hikes

Winter Months – Route accessibility depends on recent snowfall levels and temperatures. Although temperatures vary from winter to winter, trails below 4,000 feet are often pleasant for hiking. Watch for ice though. Ridge to Rivers will sometimes close foothill trails due to muddy conditions.

Spring Months – Spring is one of the best times to hike the lower elevation trails. Rivers, creeks and intermittent streams will have the most water, although you will need to use caution at some fords. Temperatures are usually mild, and wildflowers start to appear in late March and April. When it does rain in the spring, trails and dirt-surfaced roads dry faster due to the warmer daily temperatures.

Long Fork of Silver Creek in early June

Summer Months – The biggest challenge with the lower elevation hikes is high temperatures. Many of these trails have very little shade, and temperatures often reach 100° F and sometimes higher. It is best to hike in the early morning hours. Watch for rattlesnakes, too.

Fall Months – As with spring, temperatures are favorable for hiking enjoyment. Creek and water levels will be low, but many drainages will showcase beautiful fall foliage, usually in mid-to-late October and early November. Use caution during hunting season, especially on trails along the Middle Fork of the Boise River. This area receives a lot of hunting pressure in October. As fall progresses, the chance for unpleasant weather increases.

Shafer Butte, Garden Valley, Idaho City and Sage Hen Reservoir Hikes

Winter Months – Most of these hikes will not be inaccessible. Many of the trails are accessed via dirt-surfaced roads that are not maintained during winter.

Spring Months – A few of the trails might be accessible in late March and April in low snow years. By late May, except in very high snow years, nearly all the trails are accessible. Most of the hikes are near 5,000 feet in elevation and above, and wildflowers appear later, usually starting in May. Creek fords can be difficult, but water levels drop fast as spring progresses. Mosquitoes can be problematic in June. The number of people using the trails is lower than the busy summer months.

Summer Months – During the warmest months of the year, the higher elevation trails see their greatest use. River and creek flows begin to normalize. Wildflowers typically peak in June, although wildflower blooms climax on Shafer Butte and Mores Mountain in July due to their higher elevations.

Fall Months – The weather is generally stable with highs near 70° F in early fall. As the season progresses, the chances of snow and cold weather increase. Many of the trails get very little use, so your chances for solitude are good. Early October is usually the best time for fall colors. Hunting activity is high near some of the trails, especially from the second week of October until the first week of November. Make sure to wear bright colors if you hike.

RECENT FIRES IN THE AREA

Over the past three decades, there have been many significant wildfires in the Boise National Forest. One of the most recent fires (the huge Soda Fire of 2015) burned nearly 280,000 acres along the Oregon and Idaho border. Most of the area is high desert and a sagebrush-steppe ecosystem. Effects of this fire are evident on the Guffey Butte and Wilson Creek hikes.

In 2016, the Pioneer Fire charred nearly 188,000 acres north of Idaho City and Lowman. The fire devastated some areas with relatively easy hikes including Beaver Creek and sections of the Crooked River. The seven trails included in *Best Easy Hikes Greater Boise* near Idaho City and Lowman were not affected by the Pioneer Fire.

A decade earlier, the Rattlesnake Complex Fire burned northeast of Garden Valley. It impacted forest along the Devil's Slide and Peace Creek trails. The area is slowly recovering. Still older fires include the brutal 1992 Foothills Fire and the 1994 Rabbit Creek Fire. Look for recovering forest from these fires on Sheep Creek, Corral Creek and the North Fork of the Boise River.

Although a fire might be considered destructive, it is actually beneficial to a forest's ecosystem. For example, pine needles, tree branches and fallen deadwood are consumed by fire. By removing this material, more sunlight reaches the forest floor allowing grass, flowers and young trees to grow. This creates habitat

Wildflowers are one of the first species to colonize an area after a wildfire diversity. Some trees, such as the lodgepole pine that occupies more than two million acres in Idaho, require the heat from a fire to release their seeds.

It can take many years for conifers in the forest to regenerate after high-intensity fires, and you will witness the rebirth of the forest ecosystem as you hike through burned areas. Fires greatly accelerate the return of minerals to the soil and nourish new plant growth. One of the stunning phenomena of nature's recovery from fire is the colorful display of wildflowers in late spring and early summer. Wildflowers are one of the first species to recolonize an area after a significant wildfire.

Caution is advised, especially during windy conditions, when hiking in areas of standing snags because they will eventually fall, sometimes with no warning. Be particularly wary near lodgepole pine because it has a shallow root system. If you wander off-trail in burn areas, be aware of stump holes in the ground from trees and root systems burned by fire.

THE LAND

Brown-eyed Susan

Of the ten largest national forests in the United States, the Boise National Forest is the ninth largest with 2.6 million acres. It is an intricate landscape of rolling hills, deep canyons, meandering rivers and forested mountains extending north from Boise all the way to Yellow Pine in the Salmon River Mountains. Its eastern border adjoins the Sawtooth and Challis National Forests while the western border stretches from Boise to Lake Cascade. Elevations range from 2,800 feet to its highest peak the 9,730-foot Steele Mountain north of Anderson Ranch Reservoir. The area is administered by five ranger districts: Cascade, Lowman, Emmett, Idaho City and Mountain Home. There are hikes in the *Best Easy Hikes Greater Boise* from all but one (Cascade) of the ranger districts.

There are many major rivers in the Boise National Forest including the Middle and South Forks of the Salmon River, the three forks of the Payette River and the three forks of the Boise River. Several of the hikes in this guidebook explore sections of these beautiful drainages. One of the fascinating aspects of the Boise River is that the three forks collect melting snow from the Sawtooth Mountains near elevations of 10,000 feet. The three forks then plummet from the high mountains to form the Boise River that then empties into the Snake River near Parma, Idaho. From the Sawtooth Mountains to Parma, the Boise River and its three forks descend a staggering 8,000 feet. Due to the wide range of elevations, the Boise River has a variety of habitats.

About 76% of the Boise National Forest is considered forest. Common conifers found at higher elevations include ponderosa, whitebark and lodgepole pine, Douglas fir, subalpine and grand fir, Englemann spruce and western larch (also known as tamarack). Cottonwood trees, quaking aspen—the first tree to colonize an area after a burn— and willows grow along many of the steep drainages. A great number of shrubs, forbs and grasses cover the non-forested areas.

In spring and summer, there are many wildflowers to be found in the diverse topography surrounding Boise. Plant communities are determined by elevation, soil type, rainfall, winds, and northern or southern exposure. Blooms typically start in late March and early April along the Snake River and in the Boise foothills. As spring progressives, look for blooms in May to early June in the 4,000 to 5,000 foot range. Mores Mountain and Shafer Butte (the highest elevation hikes in this guide near an elevation of 7,000 feet) will normally see their blooms peaking in July.

One of the most common flowers in the area is the large, yellow-flowering arrowleaf balsamroot. This plant thrives on south-facing slopes and paints the Boise foothills with strokes of yellow in mid-spring. There are many excellent wildflower books (and apps) to help identify the many wildflowers in the region.

WILDLIFE

Wildlife is abundant in the Boise National Forest, and there are nearly three hundred terrestrial species (animals that live predominately or entirely on land) of reptiles, mammals, birds and amphibians. Large mammals include Rocky Mountain elk, mule deer, black bears, wolves, mountain lions and mountain goats. There are many smaller mammals too, including badgers, pine martens, beavers, otters, fox, hares, squirrels and chipmunks.

The likelihood of encountering a mountain lion or bear is small. If you do run into a black bear, don't run. Avoid eye contact and slowly leave the area. If you come upon a mountain lion, stay calm. Speak in a firm voice, so the animal will know that you are not its regular prey. Appear larger than you are by raising your arms above your head. Back away slowly, and make sure to give the animal a way to escape.

Birds are the most common wildlife found in the forest. Game birds include grouse, chukars, quail and turkeys. There are many species of raptors in the deep canyons. The list includes eagle, osprey, Cooper's hawk, red-tailed hawk, American kestrels, several species of owls, and northern harriers. Songbirds are plentiful along riparian creek corridors. Look for American robin, Western tanager, mountain bluebird (the state bird of Idaho) and several species of flycatchers, sparrows and warblers to name a few.

MORLEY NELSON SNAKE RIVER BIRDS OF PREY NATIONAL CONSERVATION AREA

South of the small town of Kuna is the 485,000 acre Snake River Birds of Prey National Conservation Area. This unique habitat located along the Snake River Canyon was established by Congress in 1993 to help support the greatest concentration of nesting raptors in North America. This area extends 81 miles along the deep canyon of the Snake River where crags, crevices and thermal updrafts offer the birds an ideal environment to live and raise their young. It is estimated that eight hundred pairs of raptors come to the area each spring to nest. This

A raptor's nest

includes one hundred fifty to two hundred pairs of prairie falcons, the highest breeding density in the world.

Some of the most frequently seen raptors include prairie falcon, red-tailed hawks, American kestrel, Northern harrier, ferruginous hawk (the largest hawk in North America), golden eagle, turkey vulture, rough-legged hawk and Swainson's hawk. One of the best ways to witness these raptors in the wild is to hike along the Snake River Canyon. There are four hikes in the guidebook that offer exceptional opportunities to explore this area, including Guffey Butte, Halverson Lake, Swan Falls Dam and the Snake River trails. Your best opportunity to see raptors is likely in the morning and early evening in mid-March through June. Winter is also a great season for birding as eight raptor species either winter here or use the area during winter migration.

THE PEREGRINE FUND'S WORLD CENTER FOR BIRDS OF PREY

Get nose-to-beak with raptors at the World Center for Birds of Prey, headquarters of The Peregrine Fund, a global raptor conservation organization. The Peregrine Fund's mission is to conserve raptors around the world by preventing species extinctions, protecting habitats, engaging people and addressing landscape-level threats.

At the World Center for Birds of Prey you will experience birds of prey eye-to-eye and explore the mysteries of their flight, survival and relationship with humans. Live bird demonstrations and interactive exhibits complement hands-on experiences for all ages. Enjoy panoramic views of the Treasure Valley from the interpretive trail and gazebo or browse the gift shop. All admissions, memberships/donations and merchandise purchases support raptor conservation programs worldwide. To learn more, visit peregrine-fund.org.

Snake River Canyon

Bridge over Sheep Creek (hike 38)

Twisted Spring and Spring Valley Creek (hike 1)

Fruit trees near the Polecat Trailhead (hike 4)

Currant Creek in winter (hike 3)

Peggy's Trail (hike 5)

Sweet Connie (hike 6)

22

Lupine above Stewart's Gulch (hike 8)

Grazing sheep in the Boise foothills in early April

Bridge in Hulls Gulch (hike 11)

Arrowleaf balsamroot on the Rock Garden Trail (hike 13)

24

Sunset on Shafer Butte (hike 15)

Charcoal Gulch (hike 23)

Wildflowers in July on Mores Mountain Loop (hike 16)

Mores Mountain Ridge Trail (hike 17)

Peace Creek (hike 18)

Old-growth forest along the Devil's Slide Trail (hike 20)

Long Fork of Silver Creek (hike 21)

Boiling Springs (hike 22)

North Fork of the Boise River near Short Creek (hike 24)

Bear River (hike 25)

Outcropping along Ten Mile Creek (hike 27)

South Fork of the Payette River (hike 28)

North Fork of the Boise River in June (hike 26)

Meadow and the distant Tripod Peak (hike 30)

Early October on Ten Mile Creek (hike 27)

Arrowleaf balsamroot on Warm Springs Creek hillside (hike 29)

Waterfall along the Sage Hen Nature Trail (hike 31)

Outcropping destination on Cinch Creek (hike 34)

One of the many large ponderosa pines on the Sage Hen Reservoir Trail (hike 32)

Ponderosa pine destination on Cottonwood Creek (hike 35)

View north on the way to the saddle above Logging Gulch (hike 36)

Haga Creek arrowleaf balsamroot bloom in May (hike 37)

Corral Creek (hike 39)

Rocky hillside above Trail Creek (hike 40)

Guffey Bridge (hike 45)

Swan Falls Dam hike (hike 42)

River Canyon Trail (hike 43)

Butte past Halverson Lakes (hike 44)

Jump Creek Falls (hike 47)

Juniper Gulch (hike 50)

Dago Gulch (hike 49)

Upper Leslie Gulch (hike 48)

Glossary

In the text of the guidebook, there are several words often used in the hiking world that you may not be familiar with, especially if you are new to hiking. Here is a list of simple definitions.

Ascend/ascent — to move upwards

Braided — sometimes used to describe a creek or river where it divides into several streamlets

Cairn — a mound of stacked rocks built as an indicator of trail direction. Cairns are also used to identify landmarks such as trail junctions and mountaintops.

Deadfall — a mass of fallen trees and branches

Descent/descend — to move downwards

Drainage — an area of land where precipitation collects and drains off into a common outlet, such as a larger creek, river or lake. Ravines, gulches and canyons are all drainages.

Ford — to cross a creek or river by walking or wading

Grade — an ascending, descending or level section of a hiking trail

Intermittent stream — streams that flow during certain times of the year (usually spring). Runoff from rainfall or other precipitation supplements the flow of intermittent streams.

Outcropping(s) — the part of a rock (usually large) or a group of rocks that is visible above ground

Saddle — a low point on a ridge between two summits

Scramble — walking over rough terrain

Signed junction — an intersection of two or more trails identified with a sign, usually indicating the trail's name or number

Snag — a dead tree that is still standing

Switchback — a trail that travels diagonally and then turns back on itself to gain ground up a steep slope

Talus — a mass of rock debris, usually at the base of a slope or cliff

Traverse — to cross a hill or mountain by means of a series of sideways movements from one line of ascent or descent to another

Unsigned junction — an intersection of two or more trails without any signage. Rock cairns are often used to identify the trail junction.

Author's Favorite Hikes

To help you find your ideal hike, the best hikes in nine categories are listed below. Hikes are in alphabetical order and referenced with corresponding hike numbers.

Best Forest Hikes

- **20** Devil's Slide Trail (from the north end of Peace Valley)
- **21** Long Fork of Silver Creek
- **22** Middle Fork of the Payette River
- **19** Devil's Slide Trail (from the Peace Creek trailhead)
- **31** Sage Hen Nature Trail
- **32** Sage Hen Reservoir Trail
- **28** South Fork of the Payette River
- **27** Ten Mile Creek
- **40** Trail Creek
- **29** Warm Springs Creek

Best Wildflower Hikes

- **35** Cottonwood Creek
- **37** Haga Creek
- **8** Miller's Gulch to Crane's Creek
- **16** Mores Mountain Loop
- **26** North Fork of the Boise River
- **18** Peace Creek
- **15** Shafer Butte Semi-Loop
- **27** Ten Mile Creek
- **29** Warm Springs Creek
- **30** West Mountain Trail

Best Sunset Hikes

- **9** Harrison Hollow
- **10** Lower Hulls Gulch Loop
- **50** Juniper Gulch
- **16** Mores Mountain Loop
- **4** Polecat Semi-Loop
- **3** Red Tail, Lookout and Currant Creek Trails
- **2** Seaman's Gulch Loop
- **15** Shafer Butte Semi-Loop
- **13** Table Rock Semi-Loop

Best View Hikes

- **37** Haga Creek
- **9** Harrison Hallow
- **45** Guffey Butte
- **50** Juniper Gulch
- **16** Mores Mountain Loop
- **17** Mores Mountain Ridge Trail
- **4** Polecat Semi-Loop
- **3** Red Tail, Lookout and Currant Creek Trails
- **36** Saddle above Logging Gulch
- **15** Shafer Butte Semi-Loop
- **30** West Mountain Trail

Best Easy Backpack Destinations

25 Bear River

35 Cottonwood Creek

20 Devil's Slide Trail (from the north end of Peace Valley)

22 Middle Fork of the Payette River

38 Sheep Creek Trail

24 Short Creek Trail

28 South Fork of the Payette River

27 Ten Mile Creek

40 Trail Creek

29 Warm Springs Creek

Best Fall Hikes

34 Cinch Creek

39 Corral Creek

12 Fivemile Creek

44 Halverson Lakes

11 Hulls Gulch Interpretive Trail

16 Mores Mountain Loop

18 Peace Creek

27 Ten Mile Creek

40 Trail Creek

1 Twisted Spring and Spring Valley Creek

Best Solitude Hikes

25 Bear River

34 Cinch Creek

20 Devil's Slide Trail (from the north end of Peace Valley)

37 Haga Creek

33 Macks Creek

41 Rattlesnake Spring

36 Saddle above Logging Gulch

28 South Fork of the Payette River

27 Ten Mile Creek

40 Trail Creek

Best Family Friendly Hikes

19 Devil's Slide Trail (from the Peace Creek trailhead)

12 Fivemile Creek

44 Halverson Lakes

11 Hulls Gulch Interpretive Trail

47 Jump Creek Falls

16 Mores Mountain Loop

31 Sage Hen Nature Trail

28 South Fork of the Payette River

6 Sweet Connie (first mile)

27 Ten Mile Creek

Most Challenging Easy Hikes

23 Charcoal Gulch

34 Cinch Creek

39 Corral Creek

35 Cottonwood Creek

21 Long Fork of Silver Creek

5 Peggy's Trail

4 Polecat Semi-Loop

15 Shafer Butte Semi-Loop

6 Sweet Connie

29 Warm Springs Creek

30 West Mountain Trail

Boise Foothill Overview

The foothills to the north of Boise that extend west from Lucky Peak State Park to the city of Eagle are collectively known as the Boise Front or Boise foothills. It is a land of gulches, rolling hills, finger ridges and low mountains ranging from 2,500 feet on the valley floor to the 7,582-foot Shafer Butte.

The majority of the foothills are classified as a sagebrush steppe—a semi-arid landscape characterized by cold winters and hot, dry summers. Rainfall only averages between 8 to 14 inches a year, so vegetation is primarily sagebrush, rabbitbrush and wheatgrass, although there is enough water in many gulches to sustain deciduous trees, including cottonwoods, aspen and willows. Some north-facing slopes and higher elevations support conifers, including lodgepole and ponderosa pines and grand and Douglas firs.

Most of the foothill trails are managed by Ridge to Rivers, a partnership between several government agencies and private landowners. Information regarding trail conditions, pet rules, maps, flora and fauna, etc. can be found at ridgetorivers.org. The organization produces an excellent large map of the trail system that can be purchased at most outdoor retailers in Boise.

Hikers should be aware that there are dog regulations throughout the trail system, and they are enforced. A few of the trails require dogs to be on leash at all times. Please pick up after your pet. Dog owners will find trash can and mutt mitts—essentially plastic bags—provided at most foothill trailheads to encourage pet waste removal. Please dispose of the waste in the trailhead trashcans. During winter and spring, elk and mule deer migrate to the lower foothills for food and to escape snow. They survive winter by utilizing their stored body fat, so expending extra energy if they are chased or startled by dogs or humans can hurt their chance of making it to spring. Keep control of your dog; don't let them chase wildlife.

Avoid using the trails when they are muddy because this is the leading cause of trail damage. This is especially an issue in winter and early spring when the area gets most of its precipitation. Hike in the early morning when the ground is still frozen, and walk through muddy areas when you encounter them. When you walk off-trail, you kill trailside vegetation and widen the trail. During muddy conditions, Ridge to Rivers will often close trails to prevent damage.

Some of the trails cross private property thanks to easements from landowners who grant access to the public. Please respect the rights of landowners by staying on marked trails and following trail rules. You may see cattle or sheep along some trails during certain times of the year. Do not disturb the animals.

TWISTED SPRING AND SPRING VALLEY CREEK

Distance: 4.6 miles out-and-back

Total Elevation Gain: 400 feet

Difficulty: 🚶🚶🚶

Elevation Range: 3,300 to 3,650 feet

Topographic Map: Eagle

Time: 2.5 hours

Season: March through October

Water Availability: Spring Valley Creek

Cautionary Advice: Dogs must be on leash at all times along Twisted Spring trail. The trail is open dawn to dusk. Spring Valley trail is closed November 1 to March 1.

Additional Information: amivor.com/lifesytle/trails/

Pit Latrine: Yes, at Foothills Heritage Park

Coordinates

Trailhead

N 43° 46.604'

W 116° 15.691'

Destination

N 43° 46.091'

W 116° 13.844'

TWISTED SPRING AND SPRING VALLEY CREEK

About 7 miles northwest of Boise along ID 55, you will find the small community of Avimor. The area is located at the base of the Boise foothills and contains over 100 miles of trails. Arguably, the most scenic hike is along Twisted Spring and Spring Valley Creek trails.

Starting near Heritage Park, Twisted Spring trail meanders about three-quarters of a mile through a scenic backdrop of cottonwood trees, willows, sagebrush and other flora. It then merges with Spring Valley trail, which leads east into the Boise foothills. Within a half-mile, the trail enters a classic V-shaped canyon.

The most scenic part of the hike unfolds as the trail hugs the willow-lined creek. The trail's grade is modest, and there are many beautiful rock formations along the way. There are good opportunities to spot wildlife, especially raptors and deer. Picnickers will find an array of interesting locations along the meandering Spring Valley Creek to enjoy the scenery. This is one of the better foothill hikes near Boise and the best months to experience the area are in spring and early fall.

DRIVING DIRECTIONS

From the intersection of State Street and ID 55, drive north 7.3 miles on ID 55. Turn right on W. Avimor Drive. At 7.4 miles, make an immediate left on N. McLeod Way. Continue 0.2 mile and then turn left into the large parking area at Heritage Park. The signed trailhead is on the opposite side of N. McLeod Way.

THE HIKE

From the trailhead, walk a few yards, and come to an information board with maps and rules regarding the trails. From here, continue through a dense understory of flora and come to a signed junction with the Knecht Loop trail at 0.2 mile. Continue straight on Twisted Spring trail. (Knecht trail gains 200 feet in less than a half-mile and provides very good views along a sagebrush-covered hilltop. It then descends about 150 feet back to the Twisted Spring trail in another 0.4 mile.)

At 0.7 mile, come to the signed junction with Knecht Loop trail, which is the end of the trail from the earlier junction at 0.2 mile. (If you were to hike this loop, a good option in the winter when Spring Valley trail is closed, it is a 2.3 mile hike with about 300 feet of gain from the trailhead.) Continue straight and cross a bridge over Spring Valley Creek. A few yards past the bridge, arrive at a T-junction with the Spring Valley Creek trail. Turn right (east) staying to the left at the next junction with Harlow Hollows trail. At 0.9 mile, reach a gate and enter land managed by the Bureau of Land Management.

From here, the trail enters the canyon and leaves the Avimor community. The landscape is more scenic, and it feels a lot more isolated. Pass through a recent burn area at 1.1 miles as the canyon narrows and outcroppings become more prolific. The trail stays on the north side of the creek and meanders through several curvy turns before reaching a side canyon that comes in from the north at 1.6 miles. There are outcroppings here, and this is a good mini-hike destination.

Continue east up the canyon, and finally veer left (north) at 2.1 miles. The canyon is a bit wider in this area. At 2.3 miles, the trail comes to another side drainage, which also approaches from the north. A small stream confluences with Spring Valley Creek, although the stream may be dry by summer. This is another good spot for a turnaround and the end of the hike description. Adventuresome hikers can follow the trail east for several more miles.

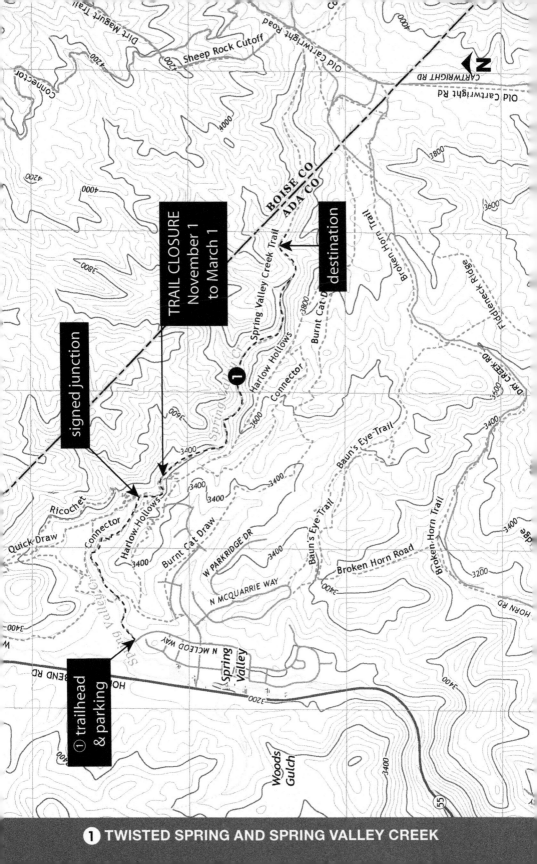

1 TWISTED SPRING AND SPRING VALLEY CREEK

2 SEAMAN'S GULCH LOOP

Distance: 2.1 miles loop
Total Elevation Gain: 250 feet
Difficulty: 🚶🚶
Elevation Range: 2,800 to 3,000 feet
Topographic Map: Eagle, Boise North
Time: 1 to 1.5 hours
Season: All year
Water Availability: None
Cautionary Advice: None
Additional Information: ridgetorivers.org
Pit Latrine: Yes

Coordinates

Trailhead
N 43° 41.617'
W 116° 16.706'

First junction with Wild Phlox Trail
N 43° 41.370'
W 116° 16.690'

SEAMAN'S GULCH LOOP

The Seaman's Gulch area is directly east of Hill Road and an easy drive from just about anywhere near the foothills. The trail system offers great views of the Boise Front Range, Treasure Valley and Owyhee Mountains. The trail is frequented by runners, hikers and mountain bikers. Although it does not see as many users as you might think considering its proximity to Treasure Valley.

The hike described combines three trails to circumnavigate the area. Along most of the route, there are beautiful views. There are several intersecting trails, which allow you to shorten the hike. Most of the trails have a nice grade, and flora is mainly sagebrush. A couple of the hillsides are southwest facing and produce a colorful arrowleaf balsamroot bloom in the spring.

DRIVING DIRECTIONS

From State Street and Gary Lane, drive north on Gary Lane. At 1.0 mile (at the intersection with Hill Road), veer left (west) as the road changes to Hill Road Parkway. At 2.2 miles, turn right into the large parking area and signed trailhead. There are two trailheads starting from the parking area. The hike is described counterclockwise, so look for the trailhead near the pit latrine.

View southwest into Treasure Valley

THE HIKE

From the trailhead, walk south about 250 feet, staying right at the first junction. The Seaman's Gulch trail parallels Hill Parkway Road passing near many large sagebrush and reaches a signed "Public Trail" junction at 0.5 mile. Veer left on the main trail, and reach another signed junction within 300 feet. Turn right on the Valley View Loop trail. (If you turn left, the Seaman's Gulch Trail climbs a ravine and soon intersects with the Valley View Loop trail.)

The Valley View Loop trail begins a gentle rise along a southwest facing slope. Sagebrush is plentiful, and you will find many bright yellow-flowering arrowleaf balsamroot in spring. As you ascend, the views of Treasure Valley become better with each step. At 0.8 mile, reach a signed junction with the Seaman's Gulch trail. Veer right and ascend nearly 200 feet over the next half-mile to a junction with the Wild Phlox trail at 1.3 miles. (If you turn left here, the trail descends 200 feet in more than a half-mile to the junction near the trailhead.)

Continue along the ridge about 400 feet to another signed junction for the Wild Phlox trail at 1.4 miles. Veer left. (If you continue on the ridge, the trail rises nearly 200 feet in 0.6 mile to a saddle and nearby knoll with very good views.) The Wild Phlox trail then descends 150 feet, weaving through sagebrush, to the trailhead in 0.7 mile.

② trailhead & parking

knoll with great views

Seaman Gulch

W LANDFILL RD

SEAMANS GULCH RD

BARNES MAIN ACCESS RD

W HILL ROAD PKWY

W PRINCE ST

ASWELL ST

N PRESCOTT AVE

ROE ST

GILLIS DR

W LAMPLIGHTER ST

GARY LN

HILL RD

Pierce Gulch

3200
3200
3300
3100
3200
2900
2900
2000
2800
3000
3100
3100
3000
2900
2900
2900
2800
2700

N

② SEAMAN'S GULCH LOOP

3 RED TAIL, LOOKOUT AND CURRANT CREEK TRAILS

Distance: 2.5 miles semi-loop
Total Elevation Gain: 400 feet
Difficulty: 🚶 🚶
Elevation Range: 2,850 to 3,100 feet
Topographic Map: Eagle
Time: 1.5 hours
Season: All year
Water Availability: Currant Creek is seasonal.
Cautionary Advice: Dogs must be on-leash at all times
Additional Information: ridgetorivers.org
Pit Latrine: No

Coordinates

Trailhead
   N 43° 43.519'
   W 116° 14.867'
First Bridge over Currant Creek
   N 43° 43.902'
   W 116° 14.794'

RED TAIL, LOOKOUT AND CURRANT CREEK TRAILS

Just north of the small community of Hidden Springs lies this wonderful hike in the Boise foothills. By utilizing an array of short trails, you can put together a great mini-loop that offers good vistas, scenic flora, a few rock outcroppings and the picturesque Currant Creek drainage.

The hike starts up Red Tail trail where you gain most of the elevation along the route. It then sidehills and climbs along Lookout trail where you get distant vistas into Dry Creek Valley. From here, it makes a short descent to a wooden bridge over Currant Creek and continues along the creek's north side, which abounds with cottonwood trees, willows and sagebrush. The final segment is back south on open hillsides to the Red Tail and Lookout trail junction.

Several of the trails do come close to a few homes, which diminishes the feeling of solitude for this hiking experience. However, since this trail system is away from the core of downtown Boise, it does not see the amount of foot traffic that trails closer to Boise see. The initial part of this hike gets very muddy after rain or snow, so avoid the hike when these conditions exist.

DRIVING DIRECTIONS

From State Street and Gary Lane, head north on Gary Lane for 5.6 miles to Dry Creek Road. (The road eventually turns into Seaman's Gulch Road.) Turn right and then proceed 1.1 miles to the signed Dry Creek Trailhead on the right (south side of road). There is plenty of parking.

THE HIKE

From the signed Dry Creek trailhead, walk a few yards and then turn left. Cross Dry Creek Road. The signed Red Tail trail starts here and winds through a switchback. After 100 feet of gain, reach a signed junction at 0.4 mile. Veer left and ascend on the Lookout Loop, which highlights expansive views down to Hidden Springs and Dry Creek Valley.

At 0.6 mile, the trail levels on a hilltop and comes to a junction signed for Currant Creek. (The trail to the right leads back to the Red Tail and Lookout junction in 0.2 mile. This is a good option for a short 0.8-mile hike.) Turn left (north), and descend an open hillside behind a row of homes staying left at the next two junctions. At 0.9 mile, cross the wooden bridge over Currant Creek. Here you will find half-buried rocks, willows and sagebrush in a little ravine. This is a beautiful setting for a break.

The trail then turns east along Currant Creek where the dense vegetation, cottonwood trees, willows and other shrubs, is especially scenic. In October, there are good autumn colors along this stretch. After a modest gain, reach a signed junction with the Red Tail trail. (The trail to the left gains more than 500 feet in 2 miles to Cartwright Road.) Veer right, and cross another bridge over Currant Creek at 1.5 miles.

Beyond the bridge, immediately turn left at the junction and then follow the signs at all other junctions for the Red Tail trail. The trail will cross two neighborhood paved roads at 1.6 and 1.7 miles. After a gain of 150 feet

and then a 50-foot descent, reach the signed junction with the Red tail and Lookout trails junction at 2.1 miles. From here, retrace your footsteps back to the trailhead in 0.4 mile.

Bridge over Currant Creek

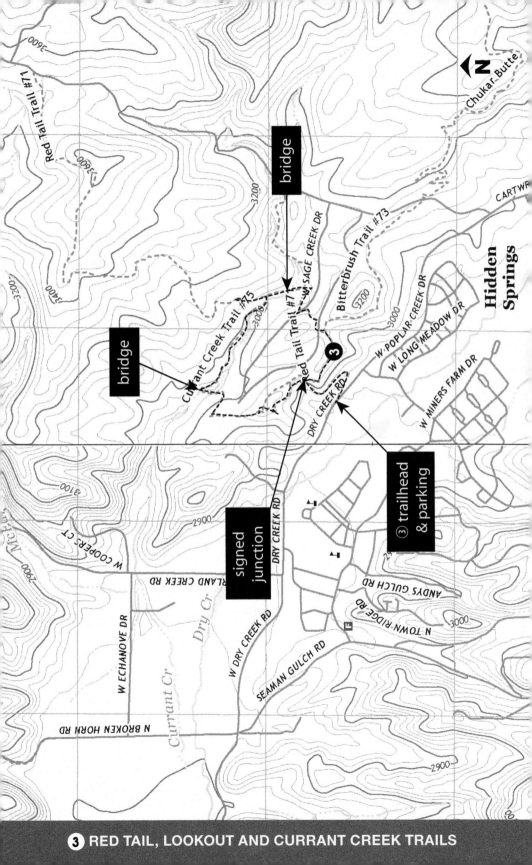

3 RED TAIL, LOOKOUT AND CURRANT CREEK TRAILS

4 POLECAT SEMI-LOOP

Distance: 3.2 miles loop
Total Elevation Gain: 600 feet
Difficulty: 🚶🚶🚶
Elevation Range: 3,000 to 3,550 feet
Topographic Map: Boise North
Time: 2 hours
Season: All year
Water Availability: None
Cautionary Advice: Dogs must be on-leash at all times. The last 0.1 mile of road is gated and closes at dusk. There is parking before the gate.
Additional Information: ridgetorivers.org
Pit Latrine: Yes

Coordinates

Trailhead
N 43° 40.545'
W 116° 14.078'
Doe Ridge and Polecat Trails Junction
N 43° 40.044'
W 116° 14.655'

POLECAT SEMI-LOOP

Considering how close you are to downtown Boise, it is remarkable how isolated you feel on this outstanding foothill trek. The trailhead is located at the base of the foothills, just a mile north of Hill Road. There is often wildlife in the area including deer, coyote, hawks, and quail. Most of the vegetation along the loop is bitterbrush, rabbitbrush, and sagebrush.

The loop ascends a gulch and gains 200 feet in less than a half-mile to a finger ridge. Once you reach the ridgetop, the trail meanders north dispensing stellar vistas of many prominent geographical features including Table Rock, the Boise skyline, Treasure Valley, the Owyhee Mountains, Lucky Peak, Doe Ridge and Shafer Butte. The route finally descends the Quick Draw Trail and returns to the trailhead via Polecat Gulch.

Like most trails in the Boise foothills, there are few trees so expect plenty of sun exposure. The trail is accessible year-round, although winter hikers should avoid the area after snowfall and rain when the trails become muddy. Dogs must be on-leash at all times on Pole-cat Gulch trails. In spring, look for the rare Aase's onion, a purple flowering plant normally found in high concentrations on south facing, sandy slopes. This is one of the few places in the world that the plant is known to exist.

DRIVING DIRECTIONS

From the junction of Hill and Collister Roads, drive north on Collister Road for 1.0 mile to the 15-stall parking lot and signed trailhead. There is a gate before entering the parking area and it closes at dusk. If the gate is closed, there is parking before the gate.

THE HIKE

The hike is described clockwise. From the signed trailhead, hike north. Within 500 feet, turn left (west) at a signed junction for the Polecat Loop. The remainder of the hike is along singletrack trail.

Continue through a stand of cherry trees, which bloom bright pink flowers in early April. Continue behind a private residence and through an area with sagebrush. At 0.3 mile, reach a signed junction. The trail straight ahead will be your return for the completion of the loop. If you

View east into Polecat Gulch

are looking for a shorter hike, continue north another half-mile to the junction with Quick Draw Trail.

To begin the loop, turn left (west) at the junction at 0.3 mile and weave through sagebrush to a switchback at 0.7 mile. The trail's grade steepens and gains 200 feet to the top of a finger ridge and veers north. It now zigzags along the ridge through large sagebrush. There are excellent panoramic views along this stretch of trail.

Reach the highpoint of the route at 1.5 miles and then begin a gradual descent of 75 feet to a signed junction with Doe Ridge Trail. (A left turn here creates a longer loop—6.4 miles—by continuing west, then north, towards Cartwright Road.) Turn right and continue another quarter-mile to a junction with the Quick Draw Trail.

Turn right again, and descend into a gulch, dropping 200 feet in a half-mile to a signed junction with the Polecat Trail. Along the descent you will see the flat-topped Table Rock in the distance. Turn right again at the junction and make a modest descent through rabbitbrush and sagebrush. In a half-mile, reach the junction you were at near the beginning of the hike. Continue south and retrace your steps 0.3 mile back to the trailhead.

Sagebrush is plentiful along the Polecat hike

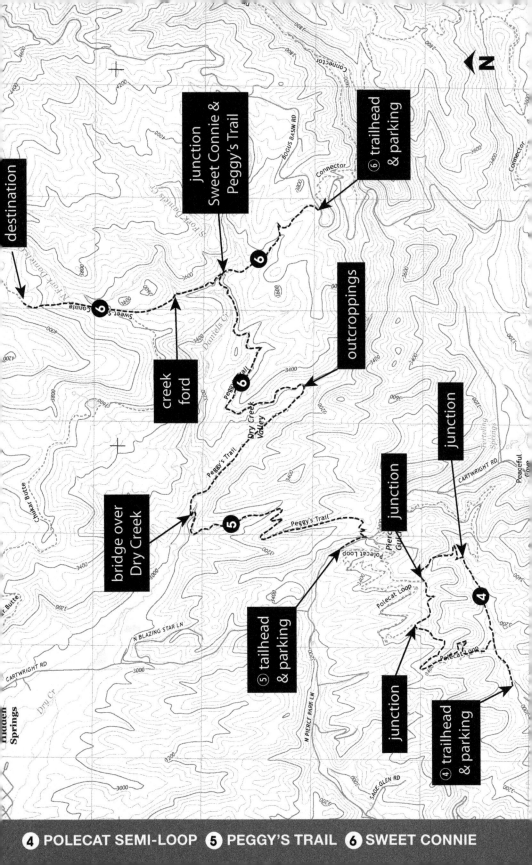

destination

junction Sweet Connie & Peggy's Trail

6 trailhead & parking

creek ford

outcroppings

junction

junction

bridge over Dry Creek

5 tailhead & parking

junction

4 trailhead & parking

4 POLECAT SEMI-LOOP **5** PEGGY'S TRAIL **6** SWEET CONNIE

5 PEGGY'S TRAIL

Coordinates

Trailhead
    N 43° 41.400'
    W 116° 13.170'
Bridge over Dry Creek
    N 43° 42.127'
    W 116° 12.748'

Distance: 4.0 miles out-and-back
Total Elevation Gain: 700 feet
Difficulty: 🚶🚶🚶
Elevation Range: 3,100 to 3,500 feet
Topographic Map: Boise North
Time: 2 to 2.5 hours
Season: All year
Water Availability: Dry Creek
Cautionary Advice: None
Additional Information: ridgetorivers.org
Pit Latrine: No

PEGGY'S TRAIL

North of Cartwright Road is the 4.8-mile (one-way) Peggy's Trail. The first couple of miles of this well-graded trail meander along open hillsides, over a sagebrush-covered ridge and down to the upper elevations of Dry Creek Valley. Here, the trail crosses a wooden bridge over Dry Creek and continues alongside the creek for about a mile before climbing out of the drainage and intersects the Sweet Connie trail, north of Bogus Basin Road.

Although this hike has a bit of elevation gain (most of it accomplished on the return), it is along a modest grade most of the way. From the trailhead, the singletrack trail travels up an open hillside and merges with a jeep road. It then meanders along a ridge offering good views of Treasure Valley and looking north wonderful vistas of the Boise Front Range. It then descends nearly 500 feet (eventually changing to a singletrack trail again) to Dry Creek.

Although the first mile of the hike has little in the way of diverse vegetation or outcroppings, it compensates with outstanding views. Once you descend into the Dry Creek drainage, this all changes. Cottonwood trees, Nootka rose bushes, willows, sagebrush, rabbitbrush, and outcroppings make for a beautiful setting near the bridge over Dry Creek. The ironically named Dry Creek flows all year and is truly one of the special places in the Boise foothills.

DRIVING DIRECTIONS

From the intersection of Hill and Bogus Basin Roads, drive north 0.7 mile. Turn left on Cartwright Road. Drive west for 2.3 miles and then turn left into the parking area for the Cartwright Trailhead. The trailhead for Peggy's Trail is on the opposite side (north) of the road from the parking area.

THE HIKE

From the signed trailhead, the trail gradually rises on an open hillside above Cartwright Road. Reach a jeep road at 0.2 mile. Veer north (left) on the old road as it zigzags to a hilltop with an elevation gain of nearly 200 feet from the trailhead. The trail stays level for a bit, passing a few sagebrush and comes to a gate and private property at 0.6 mile. You must stay on the designated trail beyond this point.

Make sure to close the gate and proceed along a finger ridge. There are far-flung views along this stretch, and at 0.9 mile, the trail rounds a hilltop with good views down to the drainage below. Although it may look a long way down, it is only about 400 feet of elevation loss to the bridge over Dry Creek from here. The trail winds through three switchbacks and veers left on a singletrack trail at 1.3 miles. The scenery improves as you make your way west beside a dry, shallow ravine. Cross the ravine at 1.7 miles and wind past a few trees and outcroppings.

At 1.9 miles, curve around a hillside where suddenly the lush Dry Creek drainage unfolds. The trail levels and comes to a little wooden bridge over Dry Creek at 2.0 miles. This is a charming setting especially in spring when the vegetation springs to life. Beyond the bridge, the level trail continues east for about a mile and then rises to a junction with the Sweet Connie trail at 4.8 miles. From here, it is 0.8 mile to Bogus Basin Road.

6 SWEET CONNIE

Distance: 4.2 miles out-and-back (Sweet Connie)
5.2 miles out-and-back (Sweet Connie & Peggy's Trail)
Total Elevation Gain: 800 feet (Sweet Connie)
550 feet (Sweet Connie & Peggy's Trail)
Difficulty: 𝄃𝄃𝄃
Elevation Range: 3,400 to 3,900 feet
Topographic Map: Boise North
Time: 2.5 hours
Season: All year
Water Availability: North Fork of Daniels Creek
Cautionary Advice: None
Additional Information: ridgetorivers.org
Pit Latrine: No

Coordinates

Trailhead
N 43° 41.500'
W 116° 10.941'
Signed Junction with Peggy's Trail
N 43° 41.973'
W 116° 11.358'

SWEET CONNIE

You can't talk about the best hiking trails in the Boise foothills without mentioning the Sweet Connie trail. It showcases beautiful outcroppings all within the first mile. In spring, the area is at its best when the hillsides are green and wildflowers bloom.

The trail starts from Bogus Basin Road and makes a moderate descent along a sagebrush-covered hillside. Just before a half-mile, you pass a few outcroppings that become more frequent and spectacular as you descend. At 0.8 mile, having descended 300 feet, you arrive at a signed junction with Peggy's Trail. There are many outcroppings, a few trees and the setting is superb for a picnic. You could turn around here if you're looking for a short, easy hike.

There are two longer hike options from the junction: You can continue north on the Sweet Connie trail and ascend, or turn west on Peggy's Trail. The Sweet Connie trail gains nearly 500 feet in more than a mile to where it levels high above the drainage. There are beautiful views looking down canyon and into Treasure Valley. The other option is to explore Peggy's Trail from the 0.8-mile junction. This route continues about 1.5 miles and descends nearly 200 feet to the Dry Creek drainage. The final destination is a striking setting among outcroppings, boulders and rocky cliffs.

Rock outcroppings near Dry Creek

DRIVING DIRECTIONS

From the junction of Hill and Bogus Basin Roads, near downtown Boise, drive north on Bogus Basin Road for 5.6 miles and then make an immediate right into the parking area. There is plenty of parking. The signed trailhead is located on the opposite (north) side of Bogus Basin Road.

THE HIKE

From the signed trailhead, descend immediately to a gate. Make sure to close the gate behind you, and remember this is private property with trail easements. Continue northwest along the sagebrush-covered hillside. At 0.3 mile, the trail winds through a switchback and soon passes a few outcroppings. Outcroppings become more frequent as you continue to descend.

After a descent of 300 feet from the trailhead, arrive at the signed junction with Peggy's Trail at 0.8 mile. There are many outcroppings and a few hackberry trees that make for a pretty setting. This is a great turnaround if you have small children or want an easy outing.

To continue along the Sweet Connie trail, turn right at the junction. (See Peggy's Trail option on the next page.) The trail meanders along a hillside and soon fords the North Fork of Daniels Creek at 1.2 miles. Continue to the signed junction with the Chukar Butte trail at 1.5 miles. (This trail leads northwest more than 4 miles to the small community of Hidden Springs.)

Continue on Sweet Connie as the trail descends to a shallow ravine and begins a 300-foot rise to where the trail levels at 2.1 miles. There are nearby outcroppings east of the trail that are a great destination. The Sweet Connie trail continues nearly 4 miles and connects with the East Side and Freddy's Stack Rock trails near an elevation of 5,400 feet.

Peggy's Trail Option

From the Sweet Connie and Peggy's Trail junction at 0.8 mile, turn left (east) on Peggy's Trail. Cross a narrow ravine and continue west above Daniels Creek. At 1.2 miles, the trail veers south for a short distance and passes through a gate. From here, continue west. Turn south on a ridge at 1.7 miles. There are very good vistas looking west into the Dry Creek drainage and beyond to Hidden Springs. The trail then descends nearly 200 feet and turns northwest at 2.6 miles near several trailside outcroppings. This is a good destination

You can continue along Peggy's Trail for another mile to a small, wooden bridge over Dry Creek. (The terrain is fairly level as the trail parallels Dry Creek.) From here, the trail continues another 2 miles, with nearly 500 feet of gain, to the Cartwright Trailhead on Cartwright Road. If you have two vehicles, this hike would make an excellent 5.6-mile one-way shuttle hike from the Sweet Connie trailhead to the Peggy's Trail trailhead.

View south from the Sweet Connie Trail

7 UPPER DRY CREEK

Distance: 4.0 miles out-and-back
Total Elevation Gain: 600 feet
Difficulty:
Elevation Range: 3,400 to 3,800 feet
Topographic Map: Boise North
Time: 2.5 hours
Season: All year
Water Availability: Dry Creek, Shingle Creek
Cautionary Advice: Poison ivy grows in sections along the creek. Use caution if you explore the creek's banks.
Additional Information: ridgetorivers.org
Pit Latrine: No

Coordinates

Trailhead
N 43° 41.306'
W 116° 10.917'
Confluence of Dry and Shingle Creeks
N 43° 42.155'
W 116° 09.238'

UPPER DRY CREEK

Contrary to its name, Dry Creek flows year-round and is one of the better foothill hikes. The trail starts from Bogus Basin Road and heads east high above Dry Creek. At three-quarter of a mile, it descends to Dry Creek, which is lined with dense vegetation including cottonwood and hackberry trees, elderberry, alder, willows and other shrubs. There is also plenty of Nootka rose, which produces bright, red berries in the fall.

As you make your way up the canyon, there are many pretty settings along the creek. The hike description ends at the confluence of Shingle and Dry Creeks where the trail splits into two drainages. There is a little wooden bridge there spanning Shingle Creek that is an excellent destination. You can extend the hike up either drainage, although the initial segment of the Shingle Creek drainage is the most attractive.

The first part of this hike traverses rocky hillsides above Dry Creek. This area is prime habitat for Crotalus oreganus, the western rattlesnake. Rattlesnakes prefer rocky terrain on south-facing slopes, and this is exactly the terrain in which this trail is located. In summer, keep pets and children close to minimize encounters. Do not let this be a deterrent though; this is one of the more beautiful hikes in the Boise foothills.

Dry Creek drainage

DRIVING DIRECTIONS

From the junction of Hill and Bogus Basin Roads, near downtown Boise, drive north on Bogus Basin Road for 4.7 miles to several pull-outs on the right side of the road. The pull-outs are immediately past a hairpin turn over Dry Creek. If the pullouts are full, additional parking is located another 0.1 mile up Bogus Basin Road.

THE HIKE

The singletrack trail starts near a small wooden fence and turns east along a gentle grade. Within 300 feet, you will come to a sign with information about the Dry Creek Watershed. The trail stays high above the drainage and arrives at a signed junction at 0.3 mile. (The trail to the left rises 200 feet in a half-mile to an alternative trailhead for Dry Creek, also located along Bogus Basin Road.) Continue east at the junction. You will soon pass a large outcropping. The trail undulates for a bit and descends to the drainage just feet from Dry Creek at 0.8 mile.

At 1.0 mile, reach the signed junction with Sheep Camp trail. (This trail leads over Dry Creek on a bridge and rises nearly 400 feet to a junction with the Hard Guy trail at 0.8 mile.) Continue northeast as the trail stays fairly level and soon crosses Dry Creek on a wooden bridge at 1.4 miles. Past the bridge, the trail skirts a grassy clearing at 1.6 miles.

The trail continues along the south side of Dry Creek and overlooks a beaver pond at 1.8 miles. After another quarter-mile of hiking, reach the confluence of Dry and Shingle Creeks. This is a nice destination. If you want to extend the hike, the most scenic option is to turn right at the signed junction for Shingle Creek. The first half-mile parallels Shingle Creek winding through a dense understory of bushes. The steep hillsides are covered with outcroppings and gnarly, hackberry trees. This trail continues just under 2 miles at which point the trail turns north and becomes very steep as it heads towards Boise Ridge Road.

Grassy clearing near the end of the hike

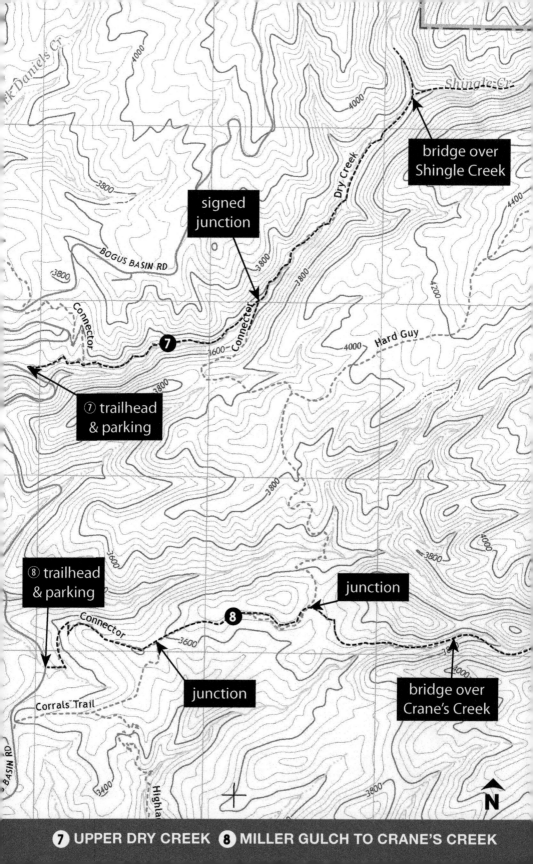

bridge over
Shingle Creek

signed
junction

⑦ trailhead
& parking

Hard Guy

⑧ trailhead
& parking

junction

junction

bridge over
Crane's Creek

Corrals Trail

Connector

Dry Creek

BOGUS BASIN RD

N

❼ UPPER DRY CREEK ❽ MILLER GULCH TO CRANE'S CREEK

8 MILLER GULCH TO CRANE'S CREEK

Coordinates

Trailhead

N 43° 40.395'
W 116° 10.792'

Bridge over Crane's Creek

N 43° 40.491'
W 116° 09.041'

Distance: 3.8 miles out-and-back
Total Elevation Gain: 500 feet
Difficulty: 🚶🚶🚶
Elevation Range: 3,350 to 3,700 feet
Topographic Map: Boise North
Time: 2 hours
Season: All year
Water Availability: Crane Creek
Cautionary Advice: None
Additional Information: ridgetorivers.org
Pit Latrine: Yes

MILLER GULCH TO CRANE'S CREEK

One of the best blooms of lupine in the Boise foothills occurs along the steep hillsides of Stewart's Gulch. The first section of this hike—almost all the gain for the hike is in the first half-mile—traverses the north-facing hillside above Stewart's Gulch and gives you great vistas of the bloom. Mid-May is usually peak bloom.

Beyond the junction with Corrals trail at 0.7 mile, the hike is along an old dirt road on open hillsides. There are excellent vistas of Treasure Valley, the distant Owyhee Mountains and the forested, rolling ridgeline of the Boise Front. The hike description ends once the trail descends into a narrow drainage and intersects with willow-lined Crane Creek. There is a little bridge over the creek, and nearby outcroppings make for a scenic setting.

Although you will see other people, it will be a fraction of the users compared to trails near downtown Boise. Sections of the trail system pass through private property. The owners have granted trail access; respect their property rights by staying on all trails.

View south into Treasure Valley

DRIVING DIRECTIONS

From the intersection of Bogus Basin Road and Hill Road near downtown Boise, drive north on Bogus Basin Road. At 3.2 miles (0.4 mile beyond the Corrals trailhead), turn right into the large parking area for the Miller Gulch trailhead.

THE HIKE

From the trailhead, the singletrack trail leads through a switchback and turns north on a west-facing hillside that has good views west. After a gain of 200 feet, turn through two more switchbacks at a quarter-mile. This is directly above Stewart's Gulch where you will find the hillsides

Bridge over Crane Creek

covered with a stunning bloom of lupine in mid-spring.

At a half-mile, you get your first views of downtown Boise and the expansive Treasure Valley and within a very short distance other notable geographical highlights including Table Rock and Shafer Butte. At 0.7 mile, come to a signed junction with Corrals trail. (If you turn right, this 0.75-mile trail descends 200 feet back to the Corrals trailhead along Bogus Basin Road.)

Turn left on the wide Corrals trail. The trail (an old road) gains 60 feet in short order and meanders to an unsigned junction at 1.0 mile. (The singletrack trail to the right parallels Corrals trail and merges back within a quarter-mile.) Continue on Corrals trail to another signed junction at 1.3 miles with the Hard Guy trail. (The Hard Guy trail goes north and intersects with the Sheep Creek trail in 1.1 miles. It then turns east and rises to 5,500 feet in 3.8 miles to the Boise Ridge Road.)

Veer right at the Corrals-Hard Guy junction, staying on the Corrals trail. The trail levels at 1.5 miles and offers excellent vistas looking south to Treasure Valley and the flat-topped Table Rock. From here, make an easy descent of 50 feet into the Crane Creek drainage. Outcroppings, the willow-lined creek and the narrow drainage make this section of the hike especially scenic. Come to a gate at 1.8 miles where there is easy access to Crane Creek. (Make sure to close it behind you.) Continue another 500 feet to a small wooden bridge over Crane Creek. This is an excellent spot for a turnaround.

Another fine destination is to continue beyond the bridge another 0.8 mile up the Crane Creek drainage. This section of trail is beautiful as you ascend nearly 300 feet to an open area. Here, the trail turns away from Crane Creek and continues to a junction with Scott's trail at 3.0 miles.

Crane Creek drainage

9 HARRISON HOLLOW

Coordinates

Trailhead
　　N 43° 38.664'
　　W 116° 12.498'
Saddle at the end of
Harrison Hollow Trail
　　N 43° 39.312'
　　W 116° 12.702'

Distance: 1.8 miles out-and-back (Harrison Hollow)
2.4 mile loop (Harrison Ridge–Who Now–Hippie Shake)
Total Elevation Gain: 200 feet (Harrison Hollow)
450 feet (Harrison Ridge–Who Now–Hippie Shake)
Difficulty: 🚶 or 🚶🚶
Elevation Range: 2,750 to 3,100 feet
Topographic Map: Boise North
Time: 1 or 1.5 hours
Season: All year
Water Availability: None
Cautionary Advice: Harrison Hollow is popular with hikers walking their dogs.
Additional Information: ridgetorivers.org
Pit Latrine: Yes

HARRISON HOLLOW

Harrison Hollow is one of the closest trail networks to downtown Boise. The wide gulch is about a mile long and braided with numerous trails. Some are along the gulch bottom while others are on the open hillsides and atop the sagebrush-covered ridgetops. This network of short trails allows you to configure many out-and-back and loop hikes.

One of the easiest hikes in the canyon is to follow the Harrison Hollow trail up the canyon. The trail is wide, and you can easily hike two abreast. Just before a mile, the trail ends on a saddle and offers good views of the surrounding hills and Boise Front.

A recommended loop and a bit more strenuous is the Harrison Ridge–Who Now–Hippie Shake Loop. This hike dishes out great vistas for most of the walk. Look to hike in early spring for wildflowers. After you hike the area a couple of times, you will get a good sense of the trail system and be able to create your own favorite routes.

DRIVING DIRECTIONS

From the intersection of Hill and Bogus Basin Roads, drive north on Bogus Basin Road for 0.1 mile. Turn left onto North Harrison Hollow Lane and continue on the road to its end at 0.1 mile. There is parking for 25 vehicles. At the trailhead there is an information board with a good map of the Harrison Hollow trail system.

THE HIKE

From the signed trailhead, head up the wide trail about 100 feet to a signed junction for the Harrison Ridge trail. (See the second paragraph to complete the loop.) If you are looking for an easy hike, follow the Harrison Hollow trail north. Pass several junctions along both sides of the trail that connect with the many trails along the open hillsides. As you make your way up canyon, sagebrush becomes more prolific. At 0.8 mile, the trail bends to the left and rises nearly 100 feet to an open saddle and signed junction with the Harrison Ridge trail. The views are very good from here. Retrace your footsteps back to the trailhead.

To complete the loop, turn right at the signed junction near the trailhead. The trail winds through a switchback and rises 100 feet to where there are superlative vistas south to the Boise skyline. The trail turns north and rises nearly another 100 feet before reaching a signed junction at 0.6 mile. (This trail leads down to the Harrison Hollow trail, which you can see below.) Continue north along the ridge as you gain another 100 feet. The trail veers left and reaches the signed Harrison Hollow trail at 1.2 miles. (If you make a hard left here, the Harrison Hollow trail descends 200 feet back to the trailhead in 0.9 mile.)

To complete the loop, follow the sign for the Who Now Loop. Reach a signed junction for the Who Now Loop trail at 1.3 miles. Turn left (south) on the Who Now Loop trail, which stays fairly level and cuts across the open hillside. At 1.7 miles, arrive at the signed junction for the Kemper's Ridge trail. Continue on the Who Now trail, which veers west, to the signed junction for the Hippie Shake trail at 1.8 miles. Turn left along the ridge, and descend more than 150 feet to another signed junction at 2.2 miles. Turn right and continue another 0.2 mile to the trailhead.

saddle

⑨

HARRISON RIDGE TRAIL

WHO NOW

Buena Vista Loop

Usery Trail

BELLOMY LN

⑨ trailhead & parking

BOGUS BASIN RD

RANCH RD

Crane Gulch

PARKHILL DR

W HILL RD

HILLWAY DR

Stewart Gulch

N ARROW VILLA WAY

N ARROW CREST WAY

PEACEFUL COVE LN

Cove Airport

Miller Gulch

N' BEC

N SIMPLOT LN

CARTWRIGHT RD

e-City Canal

N 33RD ST

N 32ND ST

N 31ST ST

N 30TH ST

N 29TH ST

N 28TH ST

N 26TH ST

GOOD ST

GAVIN ST

GRACE ST

IRENE ST

BELLA ST

DORA ST

BOISE

Connector

Red Fox Tr

WY

W B

3400

3200

3000

3400

3200

3200

2800

3000

3200

3000

3000

3000

3200

3000

2800

2800

⑨ HARRISON HOLLOW

10 LOWER HULLS GULCH LOOP

Coordinates

Trailhead
　　N 43° 38.538'
　　W 116° 11.089'
**Red Cliff and Crest-
line Trail Junction**
　　N 43° 38.387'
　　W 116° 11.925'

Distance: 3.1 miles loop
Total Elevation Gain: 500 feet
Difficulty:
Elevation Range: 2,900 to 3,400 feet
Topographic Map: Boise North
Time: 1.5 to 2 hours
Season: All year
Water Availability: Seasonal in Hulls Gulch
Cautionary Advice: None
Additional Information: ridgetorivers.org
Pit Latrine: Yes

LOWER HULLS GULCH LOOP

By combining four different trails—Lower Hulls Gulch, Red Cliffs, Crestline and Kestrel—you can create a varied and scenic loop hike only minutes from downtown Boise. The route follows Hulls Gulch for a short distance and then gains elevation up the Red Cliffs trail where you get good views of Treasure Valley and the Boise foothills. You then head southwest about a half-mile along an open ridge on the Crestline trail. The final mile is all downhill on the Kestrel trail, which takes you back to the trailhead through a sagebrush-covered gulch.

The loop is split between hiking through gulches and following ridge-lines. The open hillsides contain a variety of shrubs including rabbit-brush, bitterbrush and sagebrush. Rabbitbrush is abundant and adds color in the fall when it flowers yellow, changing to bright silver by the end of fall.

The Hulls Gulch and Table Rock areas are two of the most used trail systems in the Boise foothills, so don't expect a lot of solitude. Watch for mountain bikers who often approach too fast from the rear. If you intend to hike in summer, look to go in the early morning or late evening because the open hillsides can be brutally hot.

DRIVING DIRECTIONS

From the intersection of State and 8th Streets near downtown Boise, drive north on 8th Street for 1.8 miles to the Lower Hulls Gulch trailhead and Foothills Learning Center. (The road turns to a dirt surface at 1.4 miles.) Turn right into the parking area. The Lower Hulls Gulch trailhead is near the information board.

THE HIKE

The hike is described clockwise. From the parking area, the trail parallels 8th Street for a short distance and crosses a bridge over the seasonal creek in Hulls Gulch. At 0.3 mile, reach a signed junction with the Red Cliffs trail. (The Lower Hulls Gulch trail continues east and gains 600 feet in about 2 miles to a junction with the Hulls Gulch Interpretive trail.) Turn right on the Red Cliffs trail. It gains 100 feet to a signed junction at 0.7 mile. If you are looking for a shorter loop, turn right and turn right again at the bottom of the gulch, which is the Kestrel trail. This will take you back to the trailhead for an easy 1.1-mile loop.

The Red Cliffs trail continues along a sagebrush-covered ridge sandwiched between Hulls Gulch to the north and the gulch containing the Kestrel trail to the south. The trail's grade is modest and zigzags through a hillside with lots of large sagebrush at 1.1 miles. Continue with another 200 feet of gain to a Y-junction at 1.6 miles where you reach the high point of the hike. Veer right, and within 500 feet, merge with Crestline trail.

This trail leads southwest along a ridge, and there are good views of the flat-topped Table Rock and sprawling Treasure Valley. After about 150 feet of elevation loss, reach a signed junction with the Kestrel trail at 2.1 miles. Veer right as the trail makes a gentle descent to the bottom of the gulch and another signed junction at 2.7 miles. The trail to the right is the short spur trail that connects back with the Red Cliffs trail. Continue along the gulch bottom, passing many large sagebrush. The route is fairly level and comes to a final signed junction with the Owl's Roost trail at 3.0 miles. Veer right and reach the parking area in 500 feet.

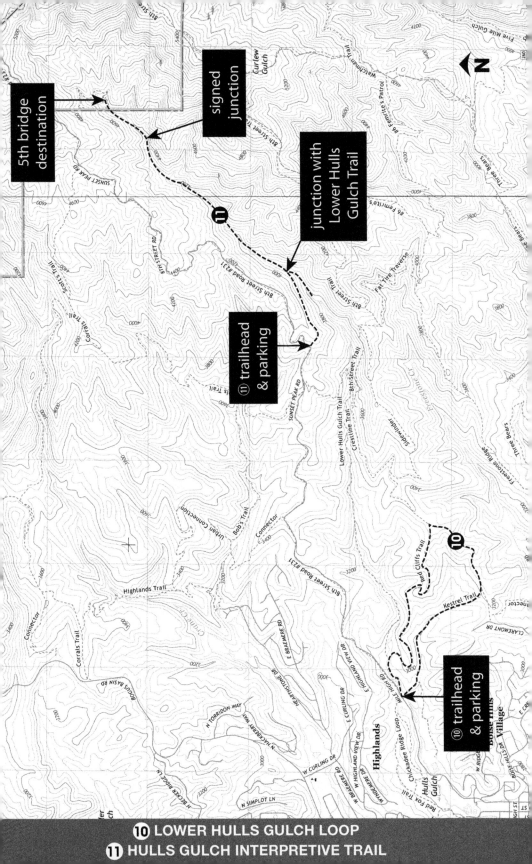

5th bridge destination

signed junction

junction with Lower Hulls Gulch Trail

⑪ trailhead & parking

⑩ trailhead & parking

⑩ LOWER HULLS GULCH LOOP
⑪ HULLS GULCH INTERPRETIVE TRAIL

11 HULLS GULCH INTERPRETIVE TRAIL

Coordinates

Trailhead
> N 43° 39.036'
> W 116° 08.600'

Fifth Bridge
> N 43° 40.109'
> W 116° 06.873'

Distance: 4.8 miles out-and-back
Total Elevation Gain: 750 feet
Difficulty: 🧍🧍🧍
Elevation Range: 3,800 to 4,550 feet
Topographic Map: Boise North, Robie Creek
Time: 2.5 to 3 hours
Season: All year
Water Availability: Seasonal in Hulls Gulch
Cautionary Advice: None
Additional Information: ridgetorivers.org
Pit Latrine: No. One is available at the 8th Street parking area 0.2 mile before reaching the trailhead.

HULLS GULCH INTERPRETIVE TRAIL

It's hard to imagine a better destination for foothill hikers than the Hulls Gulch Interpretive Trail. Although a popular area, this trail is restricted to foot traffic, greatly reducing the number of users. There are many trailside interpretive signs that provide interesting information regarding local vegetation, wildlife and geology. The hike parallels the lush Hulls Gulch for most of the route. The drainage supports a rich combination of flora including chokecherry, Wood's rose, cottonwoods, willows and syringa (Idaho's state flower).

Although the trail is usually accessible all year, the best times to hike are spring and fall. In spring when the hills are green, look for blooming wildflowers including camas, stoneseed, sticky geraniums, woodland stars and brodiaea. The seasonal creek in the drainage is usually flowing strong, and many songbirds (western tanager, yellow warbler, sparrow, goldfinch, yellow-breasted chat) flutter about the bushes. For peak fall color, look to hike in October.

The first quarter-mile provides outstanding vistas southwest into Trea-

Rock outcroppings

sure Valley and is a great location to watch the setting sun. If you are hiking in early morning or late evening, look for coyote and mule deer. The route crosses five bridges—the final bridge is the destination—as it meanders up the floor of the gulch. Any of the bridge locations make for excellent destinations to shorten the hike.

DRIVING DIRECTIONS

From State Street near downtown Boise, drive north on 8th Street for 4.6 miles to the trailhead on your right. (The road turns to a dirt surface at 1.6 miles.) There is parking for four or five vehicles. During snow and muddy conditions, the 8th Street gate is often closed at 4.3 miles. If it is closed, park at the gate and walk 0.3 mile on the road to the trailhead. You will pass the 8th Street parking area at 4.4 miles where there is a pit latrine.

THE HIKE

Beyond the wooden trailhead gate, the singletrack trail heads east across a sagebrush-covered hillside. The views are outstanding looking southwest into Treasure Valley. At 0.2 mile, the trail veers northeast high above Hulls Gulch. Make an easy descent to a signed junction at a half-mile with the Lower Hulls Gulch trail. (This trail heads southwest, connecting with other trails, and eventually leads to the Foothills Learning Center in just under 3.0 miles.)

At the junction, continue north and across the first of five bridges at 0.6 mile to where the trail starts an easy rise and reaches the second bridge at 1.0 mile. Beyond the second bridge, pass a large, hillside rock outcropping and then cross the third and fourth bridges at 1.7 and 1.8 miles respectively. After crossing the fourth bridge, you get good views of the sparsely forested ridgeline ahead. At 2.0 miles, arrive at a signed junction. (The trail to the left ascends a steep 450 feet to a junction for the Upper Hulls Gulch trailhead in 0.6 mile.)

To find the last bridge over Hulls Gulch, continue past the signed junction. The trail rises through two switchbacks and reaches the final bridge at 2.4 miles. The gulch is densely wooded in this area and makes for an excellent destination and turnaround. If you continue past the bridge, the trail rises about 350 feet to a junction for the Upper Hulls Gulch trailhead in 1.0 mile. You can then descend 450 feet back to the signed junction at 2.0 miles for a semi-loop hike.

One of the many bridges in Hulls Gulch

12 FIVEMILE CREEK

Coordinates

Trailhead
N 43° 37.838'
W 116° 06.369'

Signed Junction with the Watchman Trail
N 43° 38.800'
W 116° 05.550'

Distance: 2.8 miles out-and-back
Total Elevation Gain: 500 feet
Difficulty: 🚶 🚶
Elevation Range: 3,800 to 4,300 feet
Topographic Map: Robie Creek
Time: 1.5 hours
Season: All year
Water Availability: Fivemile Creek is seasonal. It's best to bring your own.
Cautionary Advice: None
Additional Information: ridgetorivers.org
Pit Latrine: No

FIVEMILE CREEK

Fivemile Creek is located about four miles north of the Shaw Mountain–Rocky Canyon Road intersection. This easy hike parallels Fivemile Creek and ends at a signed junction with the Watchman trail. The creek drainage is lined with locust and cottonwood trees, Nootka rose bushes and many other plants and frequented by coyote, fox, mule deer, hawks and songbirds.

The singletrack trail does not receive as much use as many of the foothill trails, probably because of the dirt-surfaced road access. Flower enthusiasts should hike in late April through May when the open hillsides are green and wildflowers bloom. For fall colors, hike in October.

Most of Fivemile Creek trail is on Boise's Noble Reserve, a 600-acre parcel of land that was gifted to the city by Allen and Billie Dee Noble in 2003. With an easy grade, a tree-lined creek and opportunities to see wildlife, Fivemile Creek is an excellent destination to explore with children.

DRIVING DIRECTIONS

From the junction of State and Reserve Streets, head north on Reserve Street. The road veers right at 0.5 mile where Reserve becomes Shaw Mountain Road. At 1.5 miles, take the left fork in the road. Continue another 3.7 miles to the trailhead, which is located on the north side of the road. (The road turns to a dirt surface and changes to Rocky Canyon Road 1.3 miles from the fork.) There is parking for three or four vehicles.

THE HIKE

From the signed trailhead on Rocky Canyon Road, walk north near the cottonwood-lined Fivemile Creek. Over the next half-mile, the trail rises 150 feet along a gentle grade. At 0.5 mile, cross a wooden bridge over the creek. Beyond the bridge, there are good views looking ahead to the wooded 5,800-foot ridgeline. Continue on the trail along the west side of the creek. Cross a tiny stream bed at 1.0 mile, which is dry most of the year. At 1.4 miles, cross another bridge over Fivemile Creek.

Bridge in Fivemile Gulch

Just beyond the bridge is a signed junction. This is the end of the hike. If you want to extend the hike, the right fork is the continuation of the Fivemile Creek trail and gains more than 400 feet of elevation in a half-mile to a signed junction with the Orchard Gulch trail.

The left fork is the Watchman trail. If you walk up the Watchman trail another 400 feet (about 50 feet of gain), you will come to a nice setting to enjoy a break. Beyond this point, the trail's grade is much steeper: It rises 300 feet to a final ford of Fivemile Creek at 1.9 miles and continues west to Femrite's Patrol trail at 4.1 miles (from the trailhead).

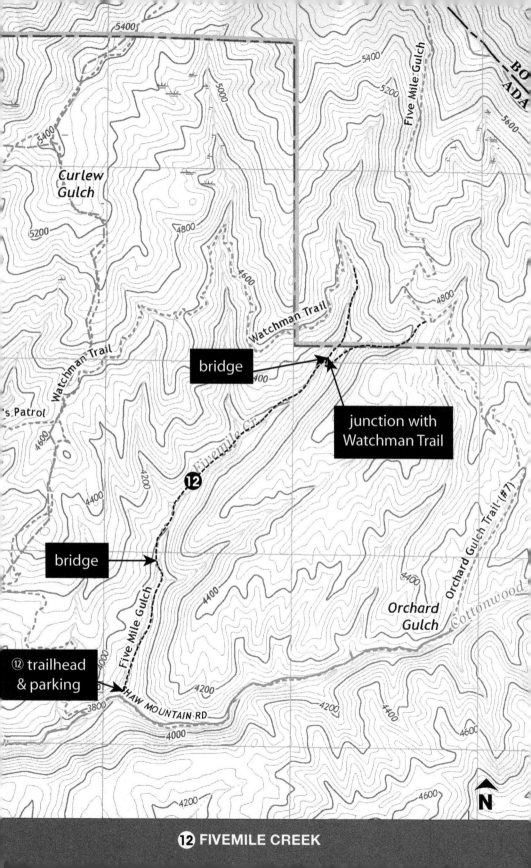

Curlew
Gulch

Five Mile Gulch

Watchman Trail

Watchman Trail

's Patrol

bridge

junction with
Watchman Trail

Fivemile Cr.

⑫

Orchard Gulch Trail (#7)

bridge

Five Mile Gulch

Orchard
Gulch

Cottonwood

⑫ trailhead
& parking

SHAW MOUNTAIN RD.

BO
ADA

N

⑫ FIVEMILE CREEK

TABLE ROCK SEMI-LOOP

Distance: 1.8 miles semi-loop
Total Elevation Gain: 400 feet
Difficulty:
Elevation Range: 2,750 to 3,150 feet
Topographic Map: Boise South
Time: 1 hour
Season: All year
Water Availability: None
Cautionary Advice: None
Additional Information: ridgetorivers.org
Pit Latrine: No

Coordinates

Trailhead
N 43° 35.522'
W 116° 09.813'
Rock Island and Rock Garden Trails Junction
N 43° 35.490'
W 116° 09.379'

TABLE ROCK SEMI-LOOP

East of downtown Boise is one of the most recognizable geological features of the city—iconic Table Rock. The 3,652-foot, flat-topped mesa has a lacework of trails that stretch along its perimeter and near its top. The majority of hikers leave from the Old Penitentiary trailhead just east of Table Rock, which is usually very busy—especially on weekends.

A better option (more scenic too) is to start your hike on Tram trail near the Warm Springs Golf Course. This moderately easy hike rises between lichen-covered boulders, gnarly hackberry trees and big sagebrush to a scenic setting with interesting rock formations. Here, you can sit on the edge of a steep hillside and enjoy the expansive views of downtown Boise and Treasure Valley. From here, the route turns east and descends a rocky hillside back to Tram trail and then the trailhead.

One of the best times to hike the area is in spring—usually mid-April to early May—when the yellow-flowered arrowleaf balsamroot blooms. This wildflower is prevalent on south-facing slopes and a beautiful complement to the rock features and other vegetation. There are many con-

Rock outcroppings on the Rock Island Trail

necting trails, so it's easy to configure many different loops and out-and-back hikes.

DRIVING DIRECTIONS

From the intersection of Warm Springs Road and Broadway Avenue, drive east on Warm Springs Road for 2.1 miles to the Warm Springs Golf Course. Turn right and park in the large parking area. The signed trailhead is on the opposite side of Warm Springs Road.

THE HIKE

From the trailhead, Tram trail (#14) starts a modest rise and turns east behind a community of homes. After a gain of 250 feet, reach a signed junction with Rock Island trail (#16B). Turn left as the trail winds through two switchbacks along a hillside blanketed with interesting rock formations. At 0.7 mile, the trail levels near a group of lichen-covered outcroppings and boulders. This is a great spot to enjoy the vistas looking into Treasure Valley.

At this point, almost all the elevation gain is finished. Continue to a signed junction at 0.8 mile with Rock Garden trail (#16A). Veer right (east) staying on Rock Island trial. Reach another signed junction at 0.9 mile. Turn right again following the sign for Tram trail.

The trail then descends nearly 100 feet to a signed junction with Tram trail at 1.1 miles. There you will find an information board with interesting details about native and invasive plants. Turn right on Tram trail, and proceed another three-quarter of a mile to the trailhead.

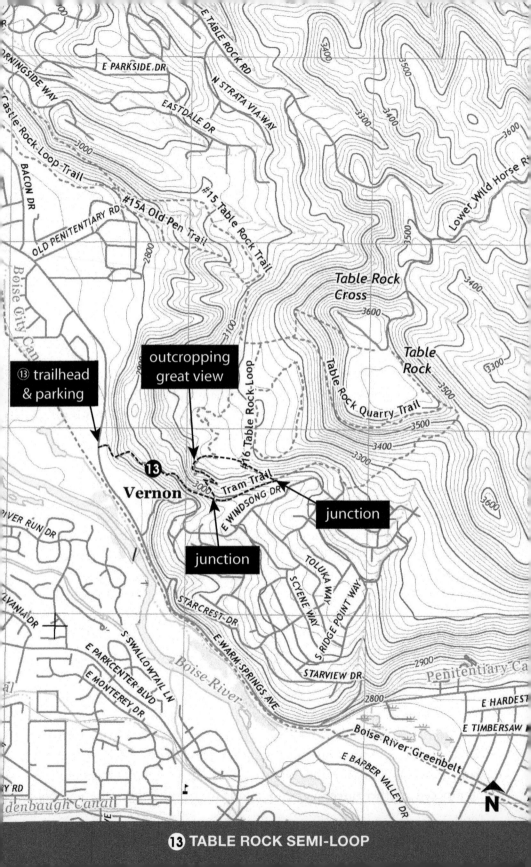

⑬ **TABLE ROCK SEMI-LOOP**

14 LYDLE GULCH

Coordinates

Trailhead
N 43° 31.197'
W 116° 03.342'

Lucky Peak Lake Overlook
N 43° 31.197'
W 116° 03.214'

Distance: 1.4 mile loop
Total Elevation Gain: 200 feet
Difficulty:
Elevation Range: 3,150 to 3,550 feet
Topographic Map: Lucky Peak
Time: 1
Season: All year
Water Availability: None
Cautionary Advice: There is little shade on the trail and it is often very hot in summer.
Additional Information: nww.usace.army.mil
Pit Latrine: Yes

LYDLE GULCH

Just south of Lucky Peak Reservoir is the often-overlooked trail system of Lydle Gulch. Most of the trails are along dirt-surfaced roads that allow hikers to walk alongside one another. There are few trees, mainly rabbit-brush and sagebrush. There are great views of Lucky Peak, the surrounding rolling hills and even the distant Treasure Valley.

This hike has a couple of options. One is an easy loop hike with a possible short, side excursion of a quarter-mile (making the hike 1.9 miles) that showcases an elevated view of Lucky Peak Lake. For a longer hike, you can continue nearly another mile up Lydle Gulch below the steep hillsides cradling the drainage.

Dog owners will be pleased because this area is off-leash. There are also two frisbee golf courses located near the trailhead. Another nice feature of the area is that there are a few metal benches scattered trailside. You won't find this type of hospitality along most Boise trails.

Lucky Peak Lake

TRAILHEAD DIRECTIONS

From the junction of Warm Springs Road and ID 21 in east Boise, follow ID 21 north for 3.0 miles, then turn right onto the paved road over Lucky Peak Dam. Proceed another 0.7 mile, and turn right at a sign for Lydle Gulch. Follow the dirt road 0.1 mile to the second trailhead. (There are two trailheads very close to one another; the first one has a pit latrine.) There is plenty of parking.

THE HIKE

Behind the gated road, follow the old road south. Just before 0.2 mile, reach an unsigned junction. The trail to the right descends a short distance and then rises 200 feet in a half-mile to a gate. There are very good views along this route. The main trail continues south, and the surrounding vegetation is thick with sagebrush and rabbitbrush. At 0.7 mile, pass a pit latrine and bench. Here, you have two options. To extend the hike, continue south up Lydle Gulch. At 0.8 mile, pass through a gate and enter land managed by the Bureau of Land Management. This public land extends approximately another 0.8 mile up the canyon before entering unmarked private property.

To complete the loop at 0.7 mile, follow the main trail as it turns back to the north and ascends 50 feet up a hillside. The trail levels for a short segment, descends past another bench and rises to an unsigned junction at 1.0 mile. Here you have a couple of options. If you want to proceed to the trailhead, turn left (north) and descend 100 feet in 0.4 mile to the upper trailhead. To see a lofty and worthwhile view of Lucky Peak Lake, turn right at the junction, and follow the road a quarter-mile (a steep 150 foot gain) to a bench overlooking the lake.

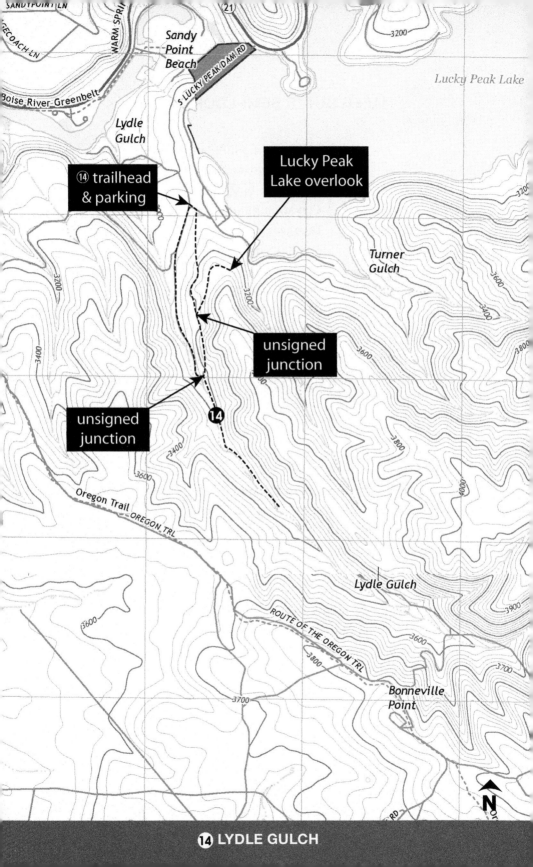

Sandy Point Beach

SANDY POINT LN

WARM SPRI

21

STAGECOACH LN

Boise River Greenbelt

S LUCKY PEAK DAM RD

Lucky Peak Lake

3200

3200

Lydle Gulch

⑭ trailhead & parking

Lucky Peak Lake overlook

Turner Gulch

3600

3200

3200

unsigned junction

unsigned junction

3600

3400

⑭

3600

3800

3800

4000

3300

3400

3600

Oregon Trail OREGON TRL

3600

Lydle Gulch

ROUTE OF THE OREGON TRL

3900

3600

3800

3700

Bonneville Point

3600

3700

RD

N

⑭ LYDLE GULCH

SHAFER BUTTE SEMI-LOOP

Coordinates

Trailhead
  N 43° 46.277'
  W 116° 06.136'
Signed Junction
  N 43° 45.727'
  W 116° 05.117'

Distance: 4.3 miles semi-loop
Total Elevation Gain: 750 feet
Difficulty: 𝄞𝄞𝄞
Elevation Range: 6,800 to 7,300 feet
Topographic Map: Shafer Butte
Time: 2.5 hours
Season: June through October
Water Availability: None
Cautionary Advice: None
Additional Information: Boise National Forest, Mountain Home Ranger District (208) 587-7961
Pit Latrine: No

SHAFER BUTTE SEMI-LOOP

Standing tall above the Treasure Valley is the largest mountain on the Boise Front: the 7,582-foot Shafer Butte. For anyone who likes to ski, the mountain needs no introduction because it is home to the Bogus Basin Ski Mountain Recreation Area. In summer, the landscape is transformed from blankets of white snow to green hillsides covered with wildflowers. Many trails and dirt roads crisscross the mountain and, depending on your aspirations, offer an array of hiking options.

One of the better outings combines the Lodge, Face and Tempest trails to create a semi-loop. This hike takes you along the south face of Shafer Butte with its numerous outcroppings and beautiful, far-reaching vistas. You continue along the east side of the mountain through a wildflower meadow and then old-growth forest. The final segment of the hike is along the shaded north side of the mountain that dispenses great views to Mores Mountain and the corrugated landscape beyond.

There are multiple trails and roads on the mountain that can be confusing for first-time users, but most are signed. Considering Shafer Butte's

View west from the Lodge Trail

easy access from Boise, it is astonishing how few people hike the area. This is a great escape in the height of summer when temperatures soar in the Treasure Valley. (It can be up to twenty degrees cooler on the mountain.) If you complete the hike and are up for another outing, hike nearby Mores Mountain. (See hikes 16 and 17.)

DRIVING DIRECTIONS

From the intersection of Hill and Bogus Basin Roads, drive north on the winding Bogus Basin Road for 15.7 miles, then enter the Bogus Basin Mountain Recreation Area. Follow the road as it veers left (turns to a dirt surface), and turn right at a sign for the Pioneer Lodge at 16.2 miles. You will pass a couple of pit latrines on your left just prior to the turn. Follow the paved road 2.0 miles to its end at the Pioneer Lodge where there is plenty of parking.

THE HIKE

From the Pioneer Lodge parking lot, head north along the west side of Pioneer Lodge. You will pass through an old tennis court and up a small hillside to a dirt road and junction with Lodge trail (#140) and Brewer's

Byway trail (#96). Continue north on Lodge trail and make a gradual climb to a signed junction at 0.4 mile with Tempest trail (#95). Turn right and begin a steep 300-foot ascent through ten switchbacks to a signed junction with the Face trail (#93) at 1.0 mile. This segment is the most strenuous section of the hike. The views are very good from the junction looking south, west and north. Turn right (south) on Face trail.

The trail stays fairly level and soon turns east along the face of the mountain. Outcroppings, summer wildflowers and the far-reaching vistas to Treasure Valley make this a very rewarding section of the hike. The ridge with the communication antennas to the southeast is Doe Point. At 1.5 miles, descend an open hillside covered in summer with wildflowers to a dirt road at 2.1 miles. Turn left, staying far right on Elk Meadows trail (#94).

Reach an unsigned junction with a road (#144) at 2.5 miles. Continue north on the singletrack trail through meadow and then old-growth forest.

At 2.7 miles, pass below chairlifts. Soon the trail veers northwest to a junction with the Lodge trail (#140) at 3.1 miles. Turn left (west) on the road, and immediately reach a 3-way junction. Veer left again, enjoying the sweeping vistas to Mores Mountain, as the road climbs nearly 100 feet and starts to descend at 3.5 miles. Continue past the Tempest trail junction at 3.9 miles. (This is the junction you were at earlier in the hike.) From here, follow your footsteps back to the trailhead.

View north to Mores Mountain

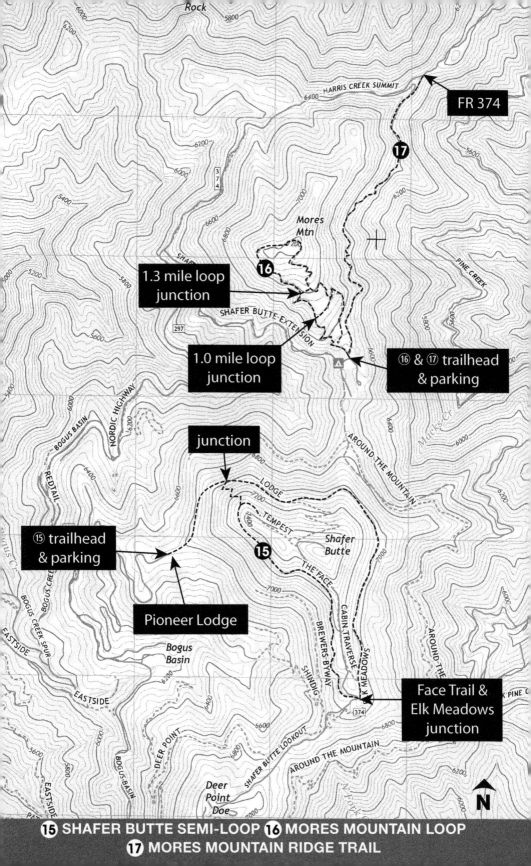

FR 374

HARRIS CREEK SUMMIT

17

Mores Mtn

16

1.3 mile loop junction

1.0 mile loop junction

16 & **17** trailhead & parking

SHAFER BUTTE EXTENSION

junction

NORDIC HIGHWAY

AROUND THE MOUNTAIN

LODGE

TEMPEST

Shafer Butte

15 trailhead & parking

15

THE FACE

Pioneer Lodge

CABIN TRAVERSE

Bogus Basin

BREWERS BYWAY

SHINDIG

K MEADOWS

Face Trail & Elk Meadows junction

374

AROUND THE MOUNTAIN

SHAFER BUTTE LOOKOUT

EASTSIDE

DEER POINT

BOGUS BASIN

Deer Point Doe

N. FORK

N

15 SHAFER BUTTE SEMI-LOOP **16** MORES MOUNTAIN LOOP
17 MORES MOUNTAIN RIDGE TRAIL

16 MORES MOUNTAIN LOOP

Coordinates

Trailhead

N 43° 47.036'

W 116° 05.15'

Highpoint of Loop

N 43° 47.458'

W 116° 05.422'

Distance: 2.2 miles loop

Total Elevation Gain: 500 feet

Difficulty: 🚶🚶

Elevation Range: 6,700 to 7,150 feet

Topographic Map: Shafer Butte

Time: 1.5 hours

Season: Mid-June through September

Water Availability: None

Cautionary Advice: None

Additional Information: Boise National Forest, Mountain Home Ranger District (208) 587-7961

Pit Latrine: Yes

MORES MOUNTAIN LOOP

Directly north of Shafer Butte you will find Mores Mountain. The 7,240-foot mountain cannot be seen from Treasure Valley because it sits behind higher 7,582-foot Shafer Butte. An old-growth Douglas fir and ponderosa pine forest covers some of the mountain, and the area is well known for the outlandish early summer wildflower spectacle along the mountain's slopes. Amazingly, more than two hundred species of plants thrive here.

The extravaganza usually begins in June with the bloom of columbine, spring beauty, wax currant and biscuitroot. By July, the meadows and hillsides are painted with yellow cinquefoil, white and maroon sego lily, pink sticky geranium, lavender lupine, red Indian paintbrush and purple penstemon. Because the hike circumnavigates the mountain, you get to see an extensive variety of wildflowers as you hike on its drier south side and the shaded north side.

Although the wildflowers are reason alone to hike the route, the remarkable and ever-changing vistas will keep you guessing about whether you should be looking up or down. Since the trail circles the high mountain near its summit, you see expansive views of Treasure Valley, the furrowed ridges surrounding Horseshoe Bend, the pointy tips of the Sawtooth Mountains and one of the best views of Shafer Butte.

There are several aspen groves on the mountain that add color during fall. Overnighters will find a small campground near the trailhead. If you are looking for a shorter hike, two cut-off trails allow you to make either an easy inner-loop hike of 1.0 mile or a bit longer middle-loop of 1.3 miles. Wildflowers, views, outcroppings and short hiking distances make this a good hike to experience with children.

DRIVING DIRECTIONS

From the intersection of Hill and Bogus Basin roads, drive north on the winding Bogus Basin Road for 15.7 miles and enter the Bogus Basin Mountain Recreation Area. The road veers left and

View south to Shafer Butte

turns to a dirt-surface (FR 297) as it climbs around the west side of Shafer Butte. (Beyond Bogus Basin, the road is open from May 15 until November 15.) At 19.0 miles, turn right on FR 374E, and follow it 1.3 miles to the Shafer Butte Picnic Area. The gated FR 374E is usually closed around September 30 and remains closed until June 15. If the gate is closed, you can walk the road to the trailhead. There is a day-use fee of $4. Just beyond the trailhead, at the end of FR 374E, is Mores Mountain Campground. There are seven tent sites, but they are very close together. They can be reserved at recreation.gov.

THE HIKE

There is no clear advantage regarding which direction you hike the loop. It is described clockwise. Near the trailhead, the trail forks. Veer left following the sign for trail #190. (The right fork is the Mores Mountain Ridge trail; see hike 17.) The trail quickly comes to a second junction. This junction—trail to the right—will be your return regardless of which of the three loops you decide to take. Continue through dense forest, and ascend two switchbacks to a junction at 0.3 mile. (For a shorter hike, turn at the junction and cross a meadow. Turn right again to create a short 1.0 mile inner loop hike.)

Continue west, passing a bench, to another junction marked with a sign "Mores Mountain Nature Trail Extension" at 0.6 mile. (A right turn quickly intersects with the outer loop trail and descends east for a 1.3-mile loop hike.) Continue straight and enter an open hillside with fantastic vistas of Shafer Butte, Stack Rock, Treasure Valley and the Owyhee Mountains. At 0.8 mile, the trail turns north and rises nearly 100 feet to where it levels again. The trail then turns along a grassy hillside on the north side of Mores Mountain and begins a gradual descent. Outcroppings and expansive views make this an especially appealing section of the hike. In summer, wildflowers are prolific.

At 1.1 miles, the trail turns south, then east and zigzags past two junctions (one for the middle-loop hike at 1.5 miles and another at 1.7 miles for the shorter inner-loop hike). After a moderate descent beyond the 1.7 mile junction, alternating between old-growth forest and small meadows with trailside benches, you will arrive at a junction marked with a trailhead sign at 2.0 miles. Turn right at the junction and walk a short distance to a final junction. Turn left to the trailhead.

There are many outcroppings along the loop.

MORES MOUNTAIN RIDGE TRAIL

Coordinates

Trailhead

  N 43° 47.036'
  W 116° 05.145'

End of Trail at Boise Ridge Road

  N 43° 48.127'
  W 116° 04.738'

Distance: 3.2 miles out-and-back
Total Elevation Gain: 400 feet
Difficulty: 🚶🚶
Elevation Range: 6,300 to 6,700 feet
Topographic Map: Shafer Butte
Time: 1.5 to 2.0 hours
Season: June through early October
Water Availability: None
Cautionary Advice: None
Additional Information: Boise National Forest, Mountain Home Ranger District (208) 587-7961
Pit Latrine: Yes

MORES MOUNTAIN RIDGE TRAIL

Beginning from Mores Mountain Trailhead, this hike traverses the east side of the 7,237-foot Mores Mountain. The trail begins near its high point and descends about 300 feet to its end at 1.6 miles at the Boise Ridge Road along the northeast side of Mores Mountain. One of the best attributes of this trail is the fantastic vistas offered along the entire route, especially looking east and north. In the distance, the corrugated views include an endless sea of ridges stretching nearly 50 miles to the Sawtooth and Trinity mountains and often-overlooked Iron Mountain. The trail is lined with occasional pines, snowbrush, willows and other plants, and there are several large outcroppings.

When the temperatures in Treasure Valley rise towards triple-digits, Mores Mountain Ridge trail is an outstanding choice to escape the heat. And, it is only 25 miles from downtown Boise. By early afternoon, temperatures drop as the sun moves to the western skyline, and the high mountaintop protects you from direct sunlight. You could combine this out-and-back hike with Mores Mountain Loop to extend your hiking adventure. (See hike 16.) Look for wildflowers in mid-to-late July including phlox, lupine, penstemon, Indian paintbrush and cinquefoil.

Mores Mountain, Mores Creek and Mores Creek Summit are named after John Marion More, a prospector in Idaho's early mining days. More was shot and killed during an argument in 1868 in the small town of Silver City. His assailant Sam Lockhart met a similar fate, although slower and likely more painful. He was shot in the arm by another prospector who saw the confrontation. Lockhart died from gangrene within a couple of weeks. The dispute that brought about the death of both men—mining claims on War Eagle Mountain.

DRIVING DIRECTIONS

From the intersection of Hill and Bogus Basin Roads, drive north on Bogus Basin Road for 15.7 miles and enter the Bogus Basin Mountain Recreation Area. The road veers left and turns to a dirt surface (FR 297), climbing around the west side of Shafer Butte. (Beyond Bogus Basin the road is open from May 15 until November 15.) At 19.0 miles, turn right on FR 374E—look for a sign for Shafer Butte Picnic Area—and proceed 1.3 miles. There is a day-use fee of $4.

Beyond the picnic area is the Mores Mountain Campground with seven tent sites—unfortunately, very close together— that can be reserved at recreation.gov. The gated FR 374E is closed around September 30 and remains closed until June 15. If the gate is closed, you can walk the road to the trailhead or continue past the junction with FR 374E another 1.6 miles to a pullout at the north trailhead for Mores Mountain Ridge Trail (signed #198). From here, you hike south to the Shafer Butte Picnic Area.

THE HIKE

A few feet from the trailhead, the trail forks. Take the right fork following the signs for trail #198. The trail makes a modest rise and passes near an aspen grove—usually peaking with fall color the first two weeks of October. At 0.15 mile, come to a signed junction with trail #190. Pass a couple of large granite outcroppings at 0.2 mile. The views east are unobstructed as you continue north.

At 0.6 mile, the trail's grade is more pronounced as it descends near a large granite outcropping abutting the trail and nearly levels at 0.9 mile. The last half-mile of the hike presents very good views looking east over the Macks Creek watershed to the mountains beyond. Reach the end of the trail along the Boise Ridge Road at 1.6 miles.

18 PEACE CREEK

Distance: 4.6 miles out-and-back
Total Elevation Gain: 650 feet
Difficulty: 🚶🚶🚶
Elevation Range: 4,500 to 5,000 feet
Topographic Map: Boiling Springs
Time: 2.5 hours
Season: Mid-May through October
Water Availability: Peace Creek, several streams
Cautionary Advice: None
Additional Information: Boise National Forest, Emmett Ranger District (208) 365-7000
Pit Latrine: Yes

Coordinates

Trailhead
N 44° 20.513'
W 115° 47.510'

Destination
N 44° 20.198'
W 115° 45.525'

PEACE CREEK

Of the four hikes starting near FR 671, the Peace Creek hike showcases the most fire impact from the 2006 Rattlesnake Complex Fire. There are a few old-growth trees still standing, and the steep hillsides are recovering nicely with saplings, snowbrush and other plants. Of the four hikes though, the Peace Creek hike certainly takes top honor for views. Along most of the hike, you get far-flung vistas up canyon and to the intriguing rock formations along the nearby 7,000-foot-high ridgeline.

The lack of dense forest allows for many wildflowers that are usually at peak bloom in late June. Peace Creek is lined with dense foliage. In late September and early October, the drainage lights up with autumn colors. The area sees few visitors during fall, so you are likely to have the trail to yourself. There are not many places to establish a quality campsite along the route as the ground is rarely level. If you want to combine a hike with an overnight stay, a good campsite is along Peace Creek at a half-mile.

Unlike the nearby Devil's Slide trail, the Peace Creek trail allows two-wheeled motorized use. Thus, it is a lot wider and sees more use. The

Bridge over Peace Creek

hike description ends just before the trail's grade becomes very steep at 2.3 miles. Here, you can hike off-trail a few yards to an open setting along the creek.

DRIVING DIRECTIONS

From the junction of ID 55 and State Street in Boise, follow ID 55 north 33.7 miles to Banks and turn right on the Banks-Lowman Road. Proceed another 8.2 miles. Turn left onto the paved Middle Fork Road (FR 698). Reset your tripmeter, and pass through the small town of Crouch. Follow Middle Fork Road to a signed junction at 14.7 miles. (The road transitions into a dirt surface at 8.5 miles.) Reset your tripmeter again, and turn right on FR 671 following the sign to Silver Creek Plunge. Follow FR 671 up and over a 5,100-foot pass for 8.4 miles to the signed trailhead on the right. There is plenty of parking. If you are traveling in early or late

View north from the Peace Creek Trailhead

season, check with Silver Creek Plunge Resort – (208) 739-3400 – to see if FR 671 is open over the pass.

THE HIKE

From the trailhead, cross Silver Creek on a bridge, and weave through open forest to a signed junction at 0.1 mile. The narrow trail to the left is Devil's Slide trail. (See hike 19.) Continue straight (east) as you enter a burn area resulting from the 2006 Rattlesnake Complex Fire. Many young trees are now growing along this stretch. At a half-mile, enter old-growth forest where you'll find easy access to Peace Creek. You could establish a camp-site here.

Rocky ridgeline above Peace Creek

From here, the trail veers northeast and begins to gain eleva-tion. Continue along a modest grade as the views continually improve looking into the canyon ahead. At 1.2 miles, turn north weaving between two tall ponderosa pines that somehow escaped the fire. The trail turns east again and gains 150 feet to where it levels on a ridge near 5,000 feet at 1.8 miles. There are good views looking down canyon. Ford two tiny streams at 2.0 and 2.1 miles. The trail starts to turn north again up a V-shaped drainage at 2.3 miles in an area that is badly burned. (See map.)

This is a good turnaround location because the route becomes much steeper beyond this point. If you venture off trail about 75 feet over dead-fall, you will find an opening along Peace Creek. There is a tiny waterfall that offers a nice spot to enjoy a break. The main trail continues up the V-shaped drainage and gains 2,100 feet over the next 4.5 miles where it connects with other trail systems leading to Tranquil Basin or Devil's Slide trail.

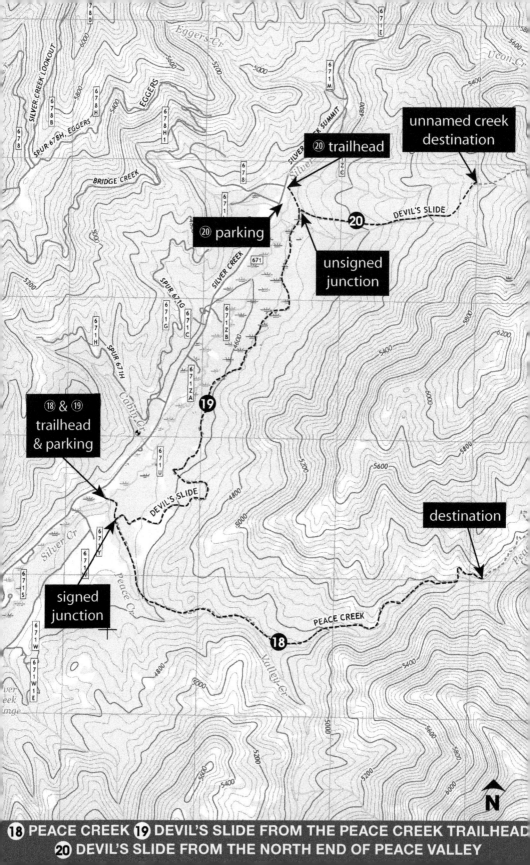

SILVER CREEK LOOKOUT

678D

678B

678H

EGGERS

SPUR 678H, EGGERS

678

678H1

678H1

Eggers Cr

671E

671M

Ucon Cr

BRIDGE CREEK

678

671

unnamed creek
destination

20 trailhead

20 parking

DEVIL'S SLIDE

20

unsigned
junction

SPUR 671G

SILVER CREEK

671

SPUR 671H

671H

671G

671C

671ZB

671ZC

CABIN CR

671ZA

19

18 & 19
trailhead
& parking

671U

DEVIL'S SLIDE

destination

SILVER CR

671Y

671V

671S

signed
junction

PEACE CR

PEACE CREEK

671W

18

671W1E

VALLEY CR

ver
reek
inge

N

19 DEVIL'S SLIDE TRAIL
(from the Peace Creek Trailhead)

Coordinates

Trailhead

N 44° 20.513'
W 115° 47.510'

Destination at Silver Creek

N 44° 21.701'
W 115° 46.506'

Distance: 5.0 miles out-and-back
Total Elevation Gain: 700 feet
Difficulty: 🚶🚶🚶
Elevation Range: 4,500 to 4,700 feet
Topographic Map: Boiling Springs
Time: 2.5 to 3 hours
Season: May through October
Water Availability: Silver Creek, Peace Creek, several unnamed streams
Cautionary Advice: None
Additional Information: Boise National Forest, Emmett Ranger District (208) 365-7000
Pit Latrine: Yes

DEVIL'S SLIDE TRAIL

If you are overdue for the restorative powers of a nature walk, strap on your hiking boots and head to Peace Valley. From the Peace Creek trailhead, this non-motorized trail leads north along the wooded slopes paralleling the three-mile-long Peace Valley that nestles the beautiful Silver Creek. Most of the route is through dense forest of spruce, pine and firs, although there are open clearings, often filled with summer wildflowers.

The trail is a beautiful singletrack that's often no more than a foot wide, adding to the off-the-beaten-path feel of the hike. You will ford several small tributary streams (most are bridged), and the trail always seems to be ascending up and over a treed hillside along a gentle grade. There are a few aspen and some huge ponderosa pines. This is a forest hike at its best.

The trail ends near the rocky-bottomed Silver Creek, an excellent destination for a picnic. If you are looking to shorten the hike, there are several bridged streams that make good turnaround points. The hike is superlative in late May and June when wildflowers bloom, and the creeks have high flows. Even so, this outing is a wonderful treat on any day the trail is accessible.

DRIVING DIRECTIONS

From the junction of ID 55 and State Street in Boise, follow ID 55 north 33.7 miles to Banks. Turn right on Banks-Lowman Road. Proceed another 8.2 miles. Turn left onto the paved Middle Fork Road (FR 698). Reset your tripmeter. Pass through the small town of Crouch. Follow Middle Fork Road to a signed junction at 14.7 miles. (It transitions into a dirt-surfaced road at 8.5 miles.) Reset your tripmeter as you turn right on FR 671, following the sign to Silver Creek Plunge. Follow FR 671. It ascends over a 5,100-foot pass and comes to the signed trailhead on the right at 8.4 miles. If you are traveling in early or late season, check with Silver Creek Plunge Resort – (208) 739-3400 – to see if FR 671 is open over the pass.

THE HIKE

From the signed trailhead, cross the bridge over Silver Creek, then continue to a signed junction at 0.1 mile. The trail to the east is the Peace Creek trail. (See hike 18.) Turn left (north) on the non-motorized trail. The narrow trail leads over a small bridge and ascends through burned forest from the Rattlesnake Complex Fire for about a quarter-mile. Saplings are flourishing here as the land recovers.

At 0.5 mile, enter old-growth forest again and gradually ascend to a bridge over a tiny stream at 0.7 mile. Turn west and descend nearly 100 feet where the trail levels again. Pass two huge ponderosa pines at 1.0 mile in open forest. The trail ascends again and nears Silver Creek at 1.3 miles. Continue north over undulating terrain. Cross bridged streams at 1.6, 1.9 and 2.3 miles. After the last bridge, enter dense forest and reach an unsigned junction at 2.4 miles. The trail to the right is the continuation of Devil's Slide trail. It leads up a steep incline and enters stunning forest. (See hike 20.)

Continue north. Arrive at a ford of Silver Creek at 2.5 miles. This is a nice setting where you can certainly spend some time. There is a trailhead on the other side of the creek near FR 671 that is the start of hike 20.

20 DEVIL'S SLIDE TRAIL
(from the north end of Peace Valley)

Coordinates

Parking Area
N 44° 21.609'
W 115° 46.572'
Unnamed Creek Destination
N 44° 21.732'
W 115° 45.449'

Distance: 2.6 miles out-and-back (distance computed from the parking area)
Total Elevation Gain: 500 feet
Difficulty:
Elevation Range: 4,650 to 5,150 feet
Topographic Map: Boiling Springs
Time: 1.5 hours
Season: Mid-June through October
Water Availability: Silver Creek, unnamed creek at the end of hike
Cautionary Advice: You will need to ford Silver Creek near the trailhead. This ford is usually passable by mid-June except in high snow years. Bring water shoes.
Additional Information: Boise National Forest, Emmett Ranger District (208) 365-7000
Pit Latrine: Yes

DEVIL'S SLIDE TRAIL

John Burroughs, the American naturalist, once quipped, "I go to nature to be soothed and healed, and to have my senses put in order." Although Mr. Burroughs was not referring to Devil's Slide trail, there may be no better place to experience his thought than this majestic forest hike. Located directly east of Silver Creek and north of Peace Valley, this spectacular outing threads through a coniferous forest full of absolutely massive ponderosa pine, Engelmann spruce and Douglas fir trees. The trees are spaced just far enough apart that only their dark-green canopies touch. Even on a bright day, very little sunlight hits the forest floor.

The hike ends at an unnamed creek adorned with moss-covered logs and rocks. Nearby, deadfall offers an ideal roost to behold this remarkable work of nature. If you seek to stay overnight in this beautiful setting, there are a few level camping possibilities about 500 feet before reaching the unnamed creek.

You can also access this area from the beginning of Devil's Slide trail, starting from the Peace Creek trailhead. Although this is a worthy hike, by starting Devil's Slide trail from this secondary trailhead, you save about 4.5 miles out-and-back to reach the unnamed creek destination. (See hike 19.) The only challenge to this hike is that you must ford Silver Creek near the trailhead. The ford is usually mid-calf in early June but drops quickly by the end of the month. Even when the water level is low, the creek is deep enough that you should bring water shoes, so you can keep your boots dry.

DRIVING DIRECTIONS

From the junction of ID 55 and State Street in Boise, take ID 55 north 33.7 miles to Banks. Turn right on the Banks-Lowman Road. Proceed another 8.2 miles. Turn left onto the paved Middle Fork Road (FR 698). Reset your tripmeter. Pass through the small town of Crouch. Follow the Middle Fork Road to a signed junction at 14.7 miles. (It transitions to a dirt-surfaced road at 8.5 miles.) Reset your tripmeter again, then turn right on FR 671, following the sign to Silver Creek Plunge. Follow FR 671, up and over a 5,100-foot pass, for 10.2 miles to a dispersed camping area with a pit latrine on the right. You could park at the trailhead, but there is room for only one vehicle. If you are traveling in early or late sea-

Old-growth forest

son, check with Silver Creek Plunge Resort – (208) 739-3400 – to see if FR 671 is open over the pass.

THE HIKE

From the parking area, head north paralleling Silver Creek. You can walk on the road or through a small clearing that has a footpath. You will come to the poorly marked trailhead with a route marker sign in about 200 yards.

From the trailhead, walk about 20 feet to ford Silver Creek. The creek is wide here, although the creek bottom is fairly rocky. After fording Silver Creek, follow the singletrack track trail about 500 feet as it veers south to an unsigned Y-junction at a quarter-

Ponderosa pines

mile. (This mileage is from the parking area.) The trail to the right leading south continues to the Peace Creek trailhead. (See hike 19.)

At the unsigned junction, veer left, and ascend a steep 60 feet to where the trail gradient is more moderate. Here, you enter a forest of giants. Huge ponderosa pines line the trail that has a grassy understory. The trail weaves under the huge canopies of trees and continues east up the hillside.

At 0.8 mile, the forest becomes denser with lodgepole pine, Engleman spruce and Douglas fir. Cross a muddy spring at 1.2 miles and soon the trail veers left (north) crossing a tiny stream. Continue another 500 feet to where the trail makes a little descent to a beautiful unnamed creek. This is the end of the hike.

The trail continues beyond the unnamed creek, but the journey is anything but leisurely. Although the beautiful ponderosa pines will be calling you to continue, note that the trail rises more than 1,900 feet in just 1.5 miles—obviously a devilish endeavor. The trail eventually connects with other trails leading to Ucon and Tranquil Basins and Peace Creek.

21 LONG FORK OF SILVER CREEK

Distance: 4.0 miles out-and-back
Total Elevation Gain: 750 feet
Difficulty:
Elevation Range: 5,000 to 5,700 feet
Topographic Map: Bull Creek Hot Springs, Wild Buck Peak
Time: 2.5 hours
Season: Mid-May through October
Water Availability: Long Fork of Silver Creek
Cautionary Advice: None
Additional Information: Boise National Forest, Emmett Ranger District (208) 365-7000
Pit Latrine: No

Coordinates

Trailhead
　　N 44° 22.955'
　　W 115° 45.512'
Long Fork of Silver Creek Ford
　　N 44° 23.519'
　　W 115° 44.202'

LONG FORK OF SILVER CREEK

Just as you know it's spring when buds form and wildflowers bloom, you can often tell a good hike by scenery found in the first few minutes along a trail. From the second you set foot under the towering old-growth forest and ascend above the cascading Long Fork of Silver Creek, the thought will occur to you that it might be worth spending some quality time here.

The hike is rarely level; the trail always seems to be rising or descending a hillside. The grades are modest though, and you will be sheltered from the sun under a canopy of trees most of the time. At 1.3 miles, there is a huge granite outcropping that hovers over the trail and is an excellent destination for a shorter hike. Beyond the outcropping, the route is fairly level and reaches a ford of Long Fork of Silver Creek at 2 miles (another worthy destination).

Although the trail is accessible to two-wheeled motorized vehicles, the rocky trail discourages use except for the most skilled riders. The canyon is very narrow, and there are no quality backpack destinations until after the first ford of Long Fork of Silver Creek. Considering the beauty of this hike, it is surprising how few hikers venture here.

DRIVING DIRECTIONS

From the junction of ID 55 and State Street in Boise, follow ID 55 north 33.7 miles to Banks. Turn right on the Banks-Lowman Road. Proceed another 8.2 miles and then turn left onto the paved Middle Fork Road (FR 698). Reset your tripmeter. Pass through the small town of Crouch. Follow the Middle Fork Road to a signed junction at 14.7 miles. (It transitions into a dirt-surfaced road at 8.5 miles.) Reset your tripmeter again, and turn right on FR 671, following the sign to Silver Creek Plunge. Follow FR 671 up and over a 5,100-foot pass for 11.9 miles to the end of the road. There are two trailheads here—Long Fork of Silver Creek and Silver Creek Summit. Make sure to turn right into the parking area for Trail 028 (Long Fork of Silver Creek). If you are traveling in early or late season, check with Silver Creek Plunge Resort – (208) 739-3400 – to see if FR 671 is open over the pass.

The Silver Creek Summit trail is much more rigorous than the first few miles of the Long Fork of Silver Creek. If you are looking for another outing, this trail leads to a lofty granite summit with sensational vistas. It is 6.4 miles out-and-back and has an elevation gain of 1,350 feet.

Huge rock wall near the end of the hike

THE HIKE

The hike starts with a steep 100-foot gain that puts you high on the north canyon wall that looks down at the cascading North Fork of Silver Creek. From here, the trail winds east and passes a large outcropping at 0.6 mile. Over the next half-mile, gain another 300 feet to where the trail levels and then descends below an enormous outcropping at 1.3 miles. The Long Fork of Silver Creek is just a few feet away, and the setting is quite scenic.

Long Fork of Silver Creek

Continue northeast and ford a couple of tiny streams. The trail stays in dense woods and finally arrives at a ford of Long Fork of Silver Creek at 2.0 miles. The forest is lush, and there are many granite boulders lining the creek. This is the destination.

If you want to extend the hike, you will need to ford the Long Fork of Silver Creek. The ford is difficult until early July. There is deadfall spanning the creek, but use caution during high water. If you do ford the creek, you will ford it three more times over the next half-mile. After the last ford, the trail becomes much steeper and rises 1,700 feet in 2.8 miles to a 7,600-foot saddle.

Waterfall on the
Long Fork of
Silver Creek

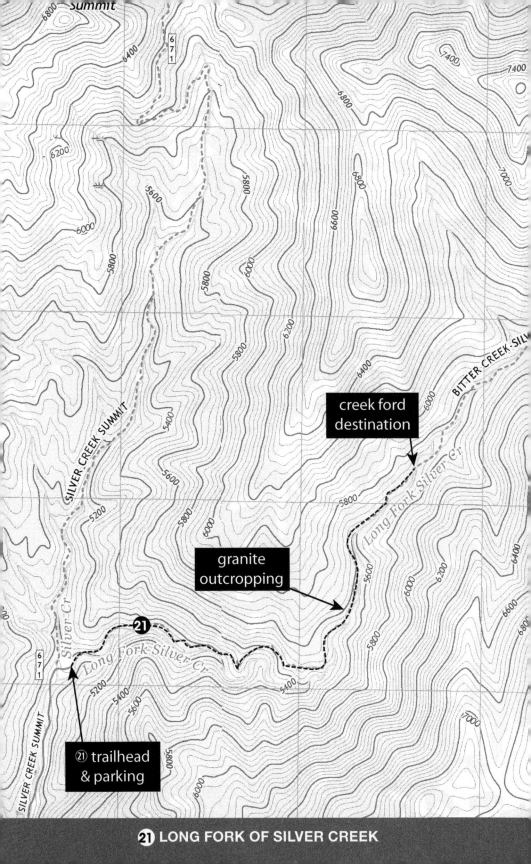

Summit

671

creek ford
destination

granite
outcropping

SILVER CREEK SUMMIT

Silver Cr.

671

21

Long Fork Silver Cr.

Long Fork Silver Cr.

BITTER CREEK-SILV

SILVER CREEK SUMMIT

21 trailhead
& parking

21 LONG FORK OF SILVER CREEK

Distance: 4.4 miles out-and-back
Total Elevation Gain: 550 feet
Difficulty: 🚶🚶🚶
Elevation Range: 4,050 to 4,200 feet
Topographic Map: Boiling Springs, Bull Creek Hot Springs
Time: 2.5 to 3 hours
Season: Late May through October
Water Availability: Middle Fork of the Payette River, Dash Creek
Cautionary Advice: There are a couple of trail sections with steep drop-offs. Therefore, this hike is not advised for small children.
Additional Information: Boise National Forest, Emmett Ranger District (208) 365-7000
Pit Latrine: No

Coordinates

Trailhead
N 44° 21.611'
W 115° 51.604'
Pine Burl Hot Springs
N 44° 22.964'
W 115° 50.597'

MIDDLE FORK OF THE PAYETTE RIVER

How about another accolade for the state of Idaho—the hot spring cornucopia of the United States. Yes, Idaho has more natural hot springs than any of the other forty-nine states. Take a journey down the Middle Fork of the Payette, and you will have the opportunity to experience several geothermal creations including Boiling, Pine Burl and Moon Dipper Hot Springs.

Hot spring allure aside, the hike along the Middle Fork of the Payette River is beautiful. The trail winds near the banks of the wide and rocky-bottomed river under old-growth forest of ponderosa and lodgepole pine. There are several locations where you can establish a campsite, and there are other camping opportunities near the hot springs.

If you are car camping, look for several dispersed campsites along the Middle Fork of the Payette River about a quarter-mile before reaching the trailhead. The nearby Boiling Spring Campground is another excellent choice with nine tree-shaded sites. You can also rent the Boiling

Springs Cabin (located just a few feet from Boiling Springs Hot Springs) at recreation.gov.

DRIVING DIRECTIONS

From the intersection of ID 55 and State Street in Boise, take ID 55 north 33.7 miles to Banks. Turn right on the Banks-Lowman Road. Continue another 8.2 miles. Turn left onto the paved Middle Fork Road (FR 698). Reset your tripmeter. Pass through the small town of Crouch. Follow the Middle Fork Road to a signed junction at 14.7 miles. (It turns into a dirt surface at 8.5 miles.) The right fork is FR 671 and leads to

Dash Creek

Peace Valley. Continue on FR 698 another 7.7 miles to the end of the road, following the signs for Boiling Hot Springs. There is parking for up to ten vehicles.

THE HIKE

From the signed trailhead, hike to a signed junction with the Wet Foot trail at 0.1 mile. Continue north (the right fork), and descend to an open hillside above the Boiling Hot Springs Cabin. Water from this hot spring is among the hottest in the state—close to 190°F. Several small trails branch to the right leading to the cabin and springs. Beyond the cabin, pass a possible campsite and then a trail sign at 0.7 mile. The trail forks here and both trails parallel the river upstream. Take the left fork because this route allows you to reach the hot springs without having to ford the river.

The trail makes a steep gain of 50 feet, high above the river, and fords a tiny stream at 0.8 mile. Over the next half-mile, the hike is fairly level until you reach a section of trail at 1.3 miles that recently washed away.

Look to your left (west) as the trail is rerouted high above the slide.

At 1.4 miles, reach an unsigned junction with the trail that forked off earlier at 0.7 mile. Continue through dense forest and across several small meadows that provide camp possibilities. At 1.9 miles, the trail enters an open area where you will smell sulfur from the hot springs. On the nearby hillside, steam rises from a small hot spring known as Lil' Dipper, but there is not enough water here to make a pool. Continue along the river passing a campsite near the confluence of Dash Creek and the Middle Fork of the Payette River. There is another campsite on the north side of Dash Creek.

To find Moon Dipper and Pine Burl Hot Springs, cross Dash Creek on deadfall. Here, turn left (west) and hike up Dash Creek. You'll come to Moon Dipper within a short distance. Here, hot water—around 135°F—oozes alongside a granite outcropping. There are several soaking pools. Pine Burl is a few more yards upstream and also features a couple of soaking pools. If you continue past Pine Burl, the foot trail fords Dash Creek and leads to good campsites in dense forest.

The main trail continues beyond Dash Creek and is lightly traveled. Horseshoe Hot Springs is another 1.5 miles away but requires five difficult river fords.

Middle Fork the Payette River

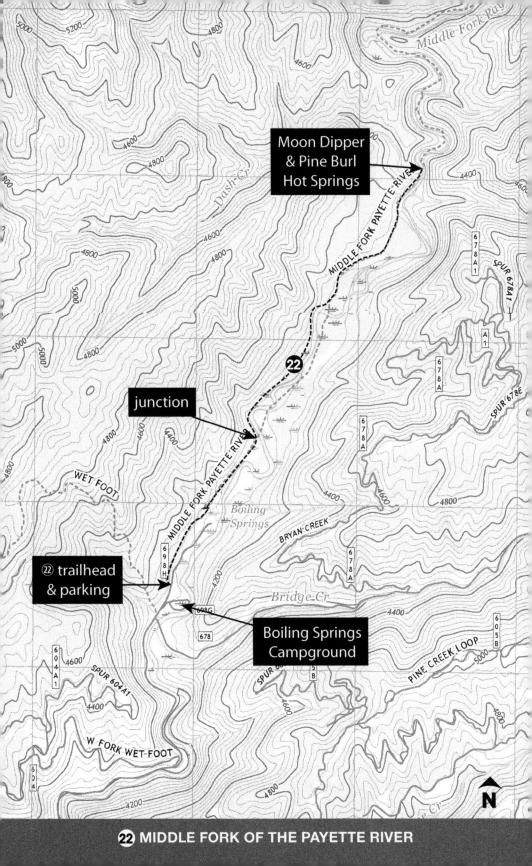

Moon Dipper
& Pine Burl
Hot Springs

junction

WET FOOT

Boiling
Springs

BRYAN CREEK

22 trailhead
& parking

Bridge Cr

Boiling Springs
Campground

SPUR 604A1

W. FORK WET-FOOT

N

23 BUENA VISTA LOOP AND CHARCOAL GULCH

Distance: 1.7 miles (Buena Vista Loop)
5.0 miles (Charcoal Gulch)
Total Elevation Gain: 50 feet (Buena Vista Loop)
950 feet (Charcoal Gulch)
Difficulty: 🥾 or 🥾🥾🥾
Elevation Range: 3,900 to 4,800 feet
Topographic Map: Idaho City
Time: 1 or 3 hours
Season: April through November
Water Availability: None on Charcoal Gulch; Elk Creek on the loop hike
Cautionary Advice: None
Additional Information: Boise National Forest, Idaho City Ranger District (208) 392-6681
Pit Latrine: Yes

Coordinates

Trailhead
N 43° 49.618'
W 115° 50.428'
Top of Charcoal Gulch
N 43° 50.564'
W 115° 52.068'

BUENA VISTA LOOP AND CHARCOAL GULCH

If you happen to be in the Idaho City area and are looking for an easy hike to stretch your legs, look no further than the Buena Vista trail. This level hike circumnavigates the dirt-surfaced Idaho City Airport—basically a single landing strip. On the first half of the hike, you'll wander through open lodgepole and ponderosa pine forest with tailings from Idaho City's mining past. The path then turns north to a bridge spanning Elk Creek. There is very little elevation gain, so hikes don't get much easier than this.

Since the trail is near the center of Idaho City and travels past a few homes, it certainly does not have the feel of an off-the-beaten-path journey. Having said that, the hike is still enjoyable, and if you are near Idaho City, driving to the trailhead isn't much of an investment. This is a great area for easy snowshoeing in the winter too.

If you have the time, there is an optional out-and back hike you should certainly attempt. About a half-mile into the Buena Vista trail, the Charcoal Gulch trail branches off to the west and ascends nearly 900 feet in 2 miles to an old Forest Service road. The primitive road, which looks like it gets very little use, is along a ridge and surrounded by forest. It is a nice destination. This hike is more remote and takes hikers through gorgeous ponderosa pine forest.

DRIVING DIRECTIONS

If approaching from the Boise area on ID 21, turn left onto Montgomery Street in Idaho City. Continue three blocks. Turn left on Wall Street. Follow this road about a half-mile to its end and the Buena Vista trailhead.

THE HIKE

From the signed trailhead, hike south in open forest. The wide trail parallels the landing strip, although trees help create a sense of isolation. At a half-mile, reach the signed junction with the Charcoal Gulch trail. (See below for a description of this trail.) Continue on the main trail, which veers south near private residences at 0.7 mile.

Leave the forest behind as the trail turns along the east side of the landing strip and passes a tiny pond with cattails, willows and a few trees. Reach a bridge over Elk Creek at 1.6 miles. Here, you have two choices. You can turn left and walk across the landing strip to the trailhead and your vehicle in 300 feet. Or, continue on the trail over Elk Creek to a T-junction with Wall Street at 1.8 miles, and turn left back to the trailhead along the road for a hike that totals 1.9 miles.

CHARCOAL GULCH

To hike Charcoal Gulch, at the signed junction at a half-mile, turn right. The singletrack trail starts a modest gain at 0.8 mile (from the trailhead) and continues through open ponderosa pine forest. At 1.6 miles, the gulch narrows into a classic V-shape, and the hike feels much more intimate. As you continue to ascend, note the increasing size of the ponderosa pine trees. The scenery remains similar until 2.3 miles. Here, the gulch widens as it approaches a broad ridge. Reach the grassy Forest Service road at 2.5 miles near an elevation of 4,800 feet.

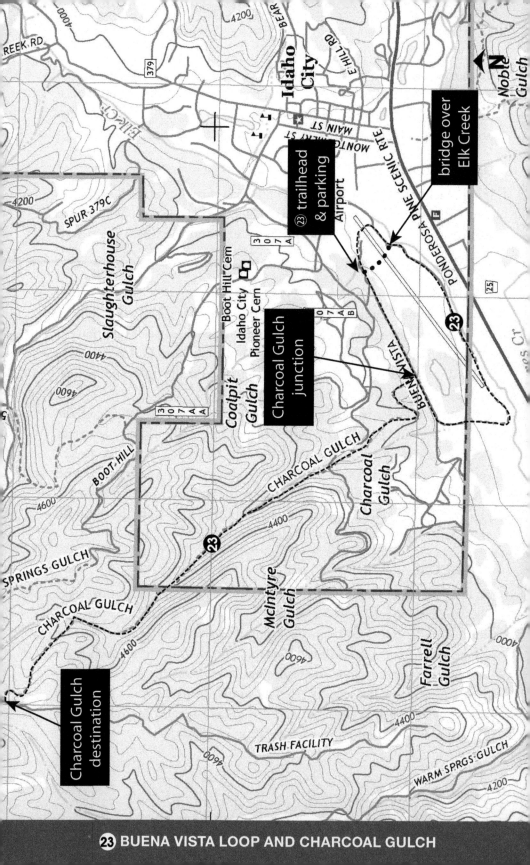

N

CREEK RD

BEAR

Idaho City

E HILL RD

379

bridge over
Elk Creek

Noble Gulch

⊕ trailhead
& parking

MONTGOMERY ST

MAIN ST

Airport

PONDEROSA PINE SCENIC RTE

F

25

-4200

SPUR 379C

Slaughterhouse Gulch

Boot Hill Cem

Idaho City
Pioneer Cem

Charcoal Gulch
junction

BUENA VISTA

23

4400

4600

Coalpit Gulch

CHARCOAL GULCH

Charcoal Gulch

Elk Cr

BOOT HILL

4600

23

4400

4600

McIntyre Gulch

Charcoal Gulch

Farrell Gulch

4000

SPRINGS GULCH

CHARCOAL GULCH

4600

Charcoal Gulch
destination

4600

TRASH FACILITY

WARM SPRGS GULCH

4200

4400

⊕ BUENA VISTA LOOP AND CHARCOAL GULCH

24 SHORT CREEK TRAIL

Coordinates

Trailhead

N 43° 47.444'

W 115° 36.186'

Short Creek

N 43° 47.958'

W 115° 36.874'

Distance: 2.0 miles out-and-back

Total Elevation Gain: 350 feet

Difficulty: 🏃🏃

Elevation Range: 3,950 to 4,000 feet

Topographic Map: Barber Flat

Time: 1 to 1.5 hours

Season: May through October

Water Availability: North Fork of the Boise River, Short Creek, Rabbit Creek

Cautionary Advice: None

Additional Information: Boise National Forest, Idaho City Ranger District (208) 392-6681

Pit Latrine: No

SHORT CREEK TRAIL

You likely don't expect much from a short 1-mile hike. But don't let the distance fool you; there is a lot to savor on this forested outing. The trail parallels the North Fork of the Boise River its entire route, often just feet from the river's edge. Along the way, ponderosa pines line the hillsides. In late spring and early summer, wildflowers dot the hillsides, too.

When temperatures rise during the summer months, you will discover clear pools in the emerald waters to escape the heat. Be careful though because the current can be stronger than it appears. Backpackers looking for an easy, yet remote setting will find unspoiled camping opportunities at the end of the hike near Short Creek. Although the hike is short, it is rarely level as it rises and falls over hillsides.

If you are looking to camp in the area, the Black Rock Campground is located a few miles east of the trailhead along the North Fork of the Boise River. There is not much privacy between campsites, but the location is beautiful with many towering ponderosa pines. Other options include renting the Barber Flat Cabin (recreation.gov) a few miles past

Black Rock Campground or dispersed camping 6.5 miles back on FR 327 near German Creek.

DRIVING DIRECTIONS

From Idaho City, drive 2.1 miles north on ID 21. Turn right onto dirt-surfaced FR

North Fork of the Boise River

327. Reset your tripmeter, and drive up and over Rabbit Creek Pass to the signed trailhead at 16.5 miles. The trailhead is on the right (south). You will need to park on the shoulder of FR 327.

THE HIKE

From the trailhead, make a quick descent of 60 feet to a ford of Rabbit Creek. There is no bridge. Fortunately, deadfall spans the creek. Past Rabbit Creek, the trail closely follows the river's edge as it meanders past outcroppings. At 0.3 mile, the trail rises nearly 75 feet above the river and continues south.

At 0.7 mile, the trail levels, and overnighters will find the flat expanse between the trail and the river to be an excellent locale for the night. There are boulders on the river's edge that make for a wonderful spot to swim in late summer. At 1.0 mile, descend to a ford of the bush-lined Short Creek. This is the destination.

If you would like to extend the hike, you have a couple of options. An easy side trip is to follow a foot trail down Short Creek and veer right near its confluence with the river. You can hike about 1,000 feet before dense vegetation and forest make travel very difficult. Another option, although hardly easy, is to continue on Short Creek trail past Short Creek. The trail starts a brutish climb through two switchbacks and gains more than a 1,000 feet in a little less than a mile to a ridge with superlative views of the area. From here, you can continue with another 600 feet of gain to a junction with Trail 689 in a half-mile.

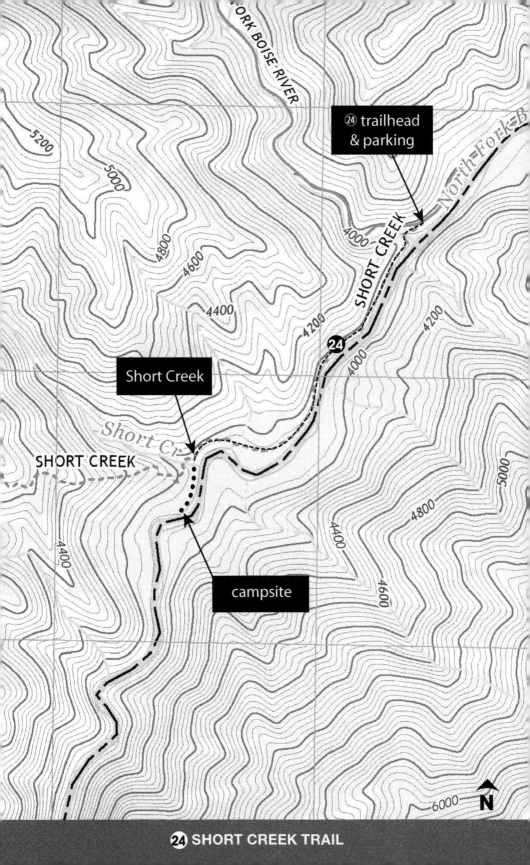

⑳ trailhead & parking

Short Creek

SHORT CREEK

campsite

24

5200

5000

4800

4600

4400

4800

4600

4400

4200

4000

4000

4200

4200

4400

4600

4800

5000

4400

6000

Short Cr

SHORT CREEK

NORTH FORK BOISE RIVER

ORK BOISE RIVER

North Fork B

N

25 BEAR RIVER

Distance: 4.6 miles out-and-back
Total Elevation Gain: 300 feet
Difficulty: 🚶🚶🚶
Elevation Range: 5,000 to 5,250 feet
Topographic Map: Bear River
Time: 2.5 hours
Season: Mid-June through October
Water Availability: Bear River, Rockey Creek, several streams
Cautionary Advice: None
Additional Information: Boise National Forest, Idaho City Ranger District (208) 392-6681
Pit Latrine: No

Coordinates

Trailhead
   N 43° 56.688'
   W 115° 27.025'
Rockey Creek
   N 43° 58.163'
   W 115° 25.482'

BEAR RIVER

With nearby river, creek and mountain names like Cub Creek, Bear Creek, Bear River and Wolf and Goat Mountains, you know the local woods are crawling with wildlife. Located on the eastern perimeter of the Boise National Forest, Bear River drains the high country located between 8,876-foot Wolf Mountain and 8,900-foot Shephard Peak. The river is a major tributary of the North Fork of the Boise River and rarely sees visitors except during hunting season.

The level hike begins near the placid Bear River in a wide glacial valley severely impacted by wildfires in the early 1990s. A few large ponderosa pines survived, and the valley is gradually recovering with willows and other plants and saplings of ponderosa pine, lodgepole pine and aspen. Within the first mile, there are several beautiful recreation spots along the river. Hikers in late June and early July will find many wildflowers.

After fording the braided Rockey Creek, you'll find your destination. Here you will discover aspen, pines, willows and plenty of level ground for a contemplative breather. If you are seeking an easy backpack, there is a good setting alongside the creek. Although this is one of the longer drives in the book, it is a worthy hike to seek out. Mention you hiked the Bear River to a friend, and they will likely just stare blank-faced at you.

DRIVING DIRECTIONS

From Idaho City, drive north on ID 21 for 17.5 miles, and turn right onto the dirt-surfaced FR 384. Reset your tripmeter. Continue 6.2 miles to the junction with FR 348. Turn left and then drive another 11.8 miles. (You will pass the trailhead for Jennie Lake at 7.3 miles.) Turn left on FR 372. This short spur road is not well marked. Immediately on your left, you will find parking. Find the signed trailhead on the opposite side of the dirt road. There are dispersed campsites along FR 348 next to the Bear River.

THE HIKE

From the trailhead, the trail wanders through a patch of old-growth forest and descends to a clearing near the Bear River at 0.4 mile. Over the next half-mile, the hike is fairly level as you pass under many large ponderosa pines. Along this segment, there are a couple of possible camping opportunities near the river.

At 1.0 mile, ford a tiny stream as the trail stays along the edge of dense forest that separates you from the Bear River. As you make your way up canyon, there are good views ahead into the canyon in which the river flows. Ford another small stream at 1.7 miles, and pass a survey marker at 1.9 miles. At 2.2 miles, the trail fizzles out in a grassy, boggy clearing. Veer right over tiny logs partially covered by high grass. After passing the boggy area—only about 20 feet wide—the trail becomes prominent again. From here, weave between aspen and conifer saplings to a ford of the shallow Rockey Creek. Although there is a primitive bridge here, its best days are behind it.

Beyond the creek, there is plenty of aspen. If you turn right (east), there are viable camp spots. Rockey Creek is your destination. Past Rockey Creek, the trail passes though snowbrush and pines and enters the narrow canyon containing the Bear River at 2.7 miles. The trail is prominent until 3.1 miles where willows encroach upon it. After a quarter-mile, the hiking gets easier and comes to a ford of the Bear River at 3.7 miles —another excellent destination if you want a longer hike.

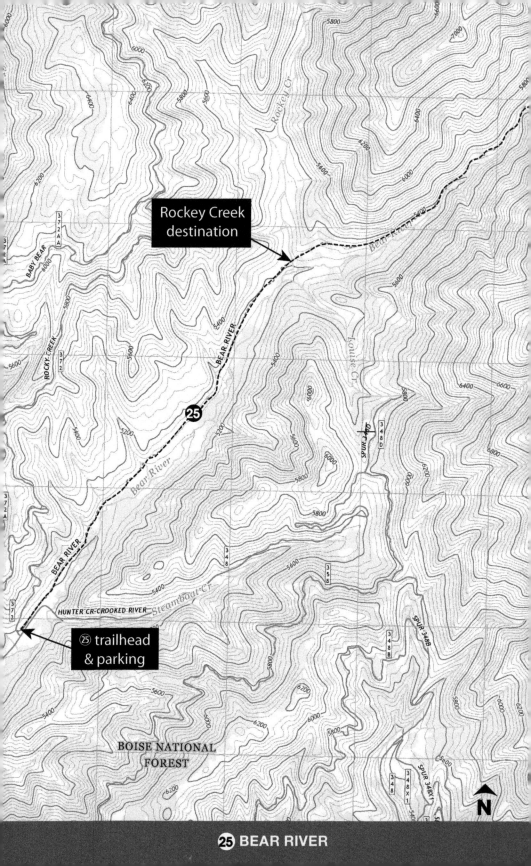

Rockey Creek
destination

㉕ BEAR RIVER

26 NORTH FORK OF THE BOISE RIVER

Coordinates

Trailhead
 N 43° 54.941'
 W 115° 24.215'
Destination along the River
 N 43° 55.328'
 W 115° 22.913'

Distance: 3.0 miles out-and-back
6.0 miles out-and-back (McNutt Creek)
Total Elevation Gain: 300 feet
600 feet (McNutt Creek)
Difficulty: 🚶🚶 or 🚶🚶🚶
Elevation Range: 4,900 to 5,100 feet
Topographic Map: Bear River
Time: 1.5 or 3.5 hours
Season: June through October
Water Availability: North Fork of the Boise River, several small streams
Cautionary Advice: Early season hikers should be aware that late spring runoff may make the route impassable at 0.8 mile due to high water. The trail's footbed is often over baseball-sized talus, so wear good hiking boots.
Additional Information: Boise National Forest, Idaho City Ranger District (208) 392-6681
Pit Latrine: No

NORTH FORK OF THE BOISE RIVER

For hikers who typically look for mountainous vistas, it's time to look lower. Bordered by steep canyon walls, a boulder-strewn riverbank and occasional sandy beaches, the North Fork of the Boise River will reward even the most ardent peakbagger. This unique landscape is some of the most spectacular river canyon scenery in Idaho.

This beautiful hike begins with a half-mile jaunt across a wooded and sagebrush-covered slope and then enters the magnificent canyon cradling the North Fork of the Boise River. The route heads north along the west bank of the river past many rapids and pools. Cottonwood, ponderosa pine and Douglas fir trees dot the riverbank and steep hillsides. In some sections, steep canyon walls rise more than 1,000 feet to jagged, high cliffs. Nothing more graphically illustrates the steep terrain than to look

125

at a map of the area.

You can end the hike at 1.5 miles where some of the most spectacular scenery is. For a more strenuous and remote adventure and a possible backpack outing, the wide section of canyon near the confluence of McNutt Creek and the North Fork of the Boise River is an excellent destination.

McNutt Creek

Near the trailhead, you can rent the Deer Park Cabin from the Boise National Forest (877) 444-6777 or recreation.gov. Car campers will find dispersed camping on both sides of the river a quarter-mile south of the trailhead. The river contains rainbow, cutthroat and bull trout. Although the hike is remarkable anytime the trail is open, late spring finds the river surging and wildflowers blooming. Early October is good for spectacular fall colors.

DRIVING DIRECTIONS

From Idaho City, drive north on ID 21 for 17.5 miles. Turn right onto the dirt-surfaced FR 384. Reset your tripmeter. Drive 13.6 miles to the North Fork of the Boise River and FR 327. Turn left following the sign to Atlanta and proceed another 5.2 miles to a signed junction. Take the left fork (FR 348); follow the sign to the North Fork Boise River Trail. Continue another 0.4 mile. Turn left at the next junction. (Going straight leads to the Deer Park Cabin.) Once you turn left at the junction, continue a couple hundred feet to the parking area on the left side of the road. The signed trailhead is on the opposite side of the road.

Destination at 1.5 miles

THE HIKE

From the trailhead, cross a sagebrush-covered hillside and come to a huge outcropping above the river at 0.4 mile. The trail veers left (north) into the canyon and descends to the riverbank near a cottonwood-sheltered beach at 0.8 mile. Early season hikers may find this section of trail underwater during high runoff years. By midsummer, when the river recedes, this is an excellent destination for a short hike.

The next section of trail is some of the most beautiful in the canyon. The trail hugs the riverbank, threading oversized talus and passing below jagged canyon walls. At 1.5 miles, come to a level section of trail perched a few feet above the river. The views looking both up and down the river are beautiful here. This is a great turnaround destination.

If you want to extend the hike, continue through a boggy area and navigate a talus slide at 1.6 miles. The trail rises and descends small hills as you continue north. The views and terrain are similar until 2.9 miles where the trail descends to a wide, level area along the river. There are a couple of good campsite possibilities near the beautiful McNutt Creek that meets with the North Fork of the Boise River. Douglas firs, ponderosa pines and a dense understory of plants make for a gorgeous setting.

The North Fork of the Boise River in June

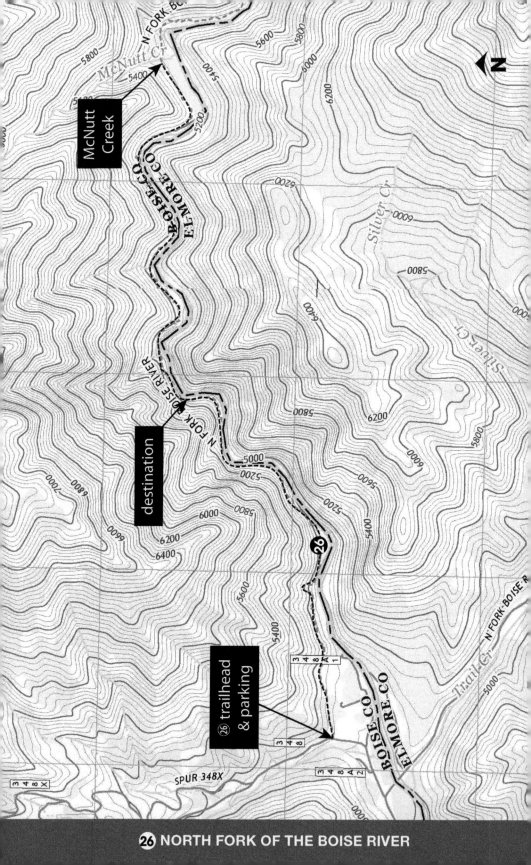

McNutt Creek

destination

26 trailhead & parking

SPUR 348X

BOISE CO
ELMORE CO

27 TEN MILE CREEK

Distance: 4.2 miles out-and-back
Total Elevation Gain: 450 feet
Difficulty: 🚶🚶🚶
Elevation Range: 4,400 to 4,800 feet
Topographic Map: Jackson Peak
Time: 2.5 hours
Season: Mid-April through early November
Water Availability: Ten Mile Creek
Cautionary Advice: None
Additional Information: Boise National Forest, Lowman Ranger District (208) 365-7000
Pit Latrine: No

Coordinates

Trailhead
N 44° 07.125'
W 115° 23.222'
Ten Mile Creek Ford
N 44° 05.509'
W 115° 22.589'

TEN MILE CREEK

If you spend a few hours hiking along Ten Mile Creek, you'll gain a better appreciation for the alluring scenery found near the community of Lowman. This easy hike begins near the confluence of Ten Mile Creek with the South Fork of the Payette River and heads upstream for several miles. Along the way, the trail wanders through a beautiful forest of pine, fir and cottonwoods and near several notable outcroppings. The route is shaded much of the way, and there are many places to sit creekside and enjoy the setting.

The willow and bush-lined creek is almost always near the trail. Although the trail is beautiful to hike anytime it is snow-free, there are two optimal times. One is late spring when the wildflower bloom is at its peak. The west-facing canyon slopes are a storybook setting when arrowleaf balsamroot paints the hillsides bright yellow. Other wildflowers grow along the canyon floor, and the drainage comes alive with a multitude of blooming bushes. The other time is usually the first week of October when the foliage transforms to beautiful fall colors.

Backpackers will find several secluded areas to set up camp for the night. One of the prime destinations is near the unsigned junction at 0.6 mile where many large ponderosa pines along the creek provide a nice canopy. The other destination is at the end of the hike along the east bank of Ten Mile Creek. Not many people know about this beautiful trail, and solitude will likely be a constant.

DRIVING DIRECTIONS

From the junction of the Banks-Lowman Highway and ID 21, travel east on ID 21 for 12.6 miles. Turn right on Ten Mile Road (FR 531). Reset your tripmeter, and drive 0.2 mile to a fork in the road. Take the left fork. (The road will turn to a dirt surface.) At 1.0 mile, turn left on a spur road. (There will be a sign for the Ten Mile trail.) Follow the rough road—passable with a passenger car—to its end and the signed trailhead at 1.2 miles. There is dispersed camping directly west of the trailhead along the South Fork of the Payette River.

Ten Mile Creek

Rock outcropping above Ten Mile Creek

THE HIKE

From the signed trailhead, walk a little over 0.1 mile to a new bridge over Ten Mile Creek. From here, the trail veers south and parallels Ten Mile Creek. Cross two wooded knolls and then come to an unsigned junction at 0.6 mile. (The trail to the left is Ten Mile Ridge trail, which gains nearly 3,500 feet in 4.7 miles to the top of Ten Mile Ridge. This is anything but an easy hike but one certainly worth the effort.)

At the unsigned junction, continue south along Ten Mile Creek. The trail begins a gentle climb through open forest. Over the next quarter-mile, spring hikers will see many blooming wildflowers. The west-facing hillside above the trail is completely blanketed with arrowleaf balsamroot in May and is a sight to see if you hit the bloom at its peak. At 1.0 mile, pass directly beneath an impressive outcropping.

From here, the trail rises another 50 feet and turns west to another unsigned junction at 1.3 miles just south of the creek. Turn left (south) on an old roadbed. Reenter dense forest and then pass below another outcropping at 1.5 miles at a sharp bend in Ten Mile Creek.

At 1.7 miles, you will come to a little clearing and a hot spring. In spring, the creek's level is usually too high to sit in the small, creekside pools. The trail continues south and at 2.1 miles comes to a ford of Ten Mile Creek, which is dangerous in early season. This is the end of the hike. Backpackers can establish a campsite here. Beyond Ten Mile Creek, the trail is very overgrown.

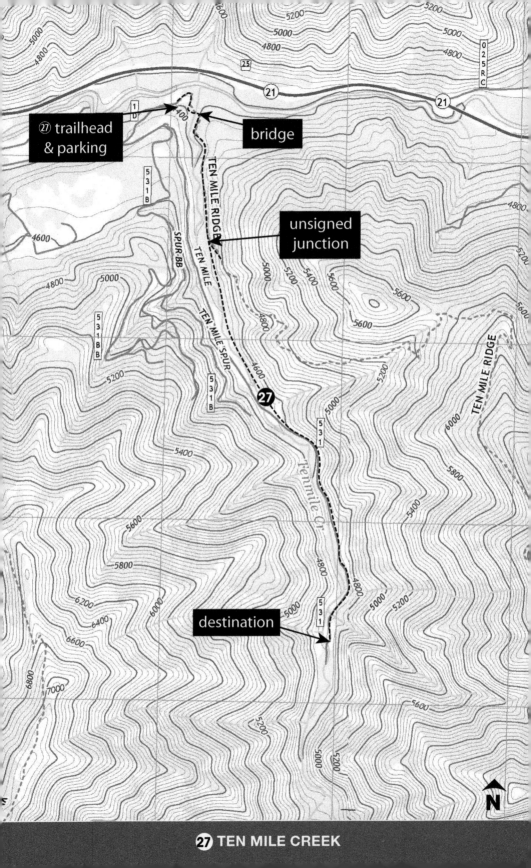

27 trailhead & parking

bridge

unsigned junction

destination

27 TEN MILE CREEK

28 SOUTH FORK OF THE PAYETTE RIVER

Coordinates

Trailhead
> N 44° 08.211'
> W 115° 18.625'

**"Lollipop Loop"
Junction**
> N 44° 09.523'
> W 115° 16.906'

Distance: 5.0 miles out-and-back
Total Elevation Gain: 400 feet
Difficulty: 🚶🚶🚶
Elevation Range: 4,600 feet to 4,850 feet
Topographic Map: Eightmile Mountain
Time: 2.5 to 3 hours
Season: Late April through early November
Water Availability: South Fork of the Payette River, several creeks
Cautionary Advice: None
Additional Information: Boise National Forest, Lowman Ranger District (208) 259-3361
Pit Latrine: No

SOUTH FORK OF THE PAYETTE RIVER

When visiting the city of Stanley from Treasure Valley, most people drive ID 21—a beautiful roadway paralleling the South Fork of the Payette River a segment of the way. Unfortunately, the river is usually only experienced as a visual second-thought. Make no mistake, this lovely hike will give you a new respect for this remarkably unspoiled river. Its banks are lined with old-growth ponderosa pines, and the river offers a captivating mix of boulder-dotted rapids, emerald-green pools and rocky-bottomed flats.

The South Fork of the Payette River finds its headwaters on the western slopes of the Sawtooth Mountains and generally flows east to west through Grandjean, Lowman and, finally, to its confluence with the Middle Fork of the Payette River in Garden Valley. Although it has not been designated a Wild & Scenic River, it probably should be because of its remarkable scenic, geological and cultural resource values. If asked, many serious anglers will say that the South Fork of the Payette River is quite possibly the best dry fly river in Idaho.

This hike parallels the river for about 2 miles and makes a little "lollipop loop" at its end. The river is always close to the trail, and there are several picturesque locations to catch a swim in the gin-clear waters during summer. Because of the low elevation, the hike is accessible in spring when the water is wicked cold and the current too strong to swim safely. There are a couple of pleasant, level grassy locations to establish a campsite under big ponderosa pines. The only negative to the hike is that you can hear vehicle traffic from ID 21, which is located on the opposite side of the river. If you hike in the spring, the river is so thunderous you'll only be able to hear it and your thoughts.

DRIVING DIRECTIONS

From the junction of the Banks-Lowman Highway and ID 21, drive east on ID 21 for 18.2 miles to mile marker 91. The trailhead is on the right (south) just before the bridge over the South Fork of the Payette River. There is parking for several vehicles at the trailhead, or you can continue over the bridge to where there is additional parking alongside the road.

THE HIKE

From the trailhead, head south into lodgepole and ponderosa pine forest. The trail turns east, paralleling the river in dense woods. At 0.3 mile, walk through a small clearing and then continue along relatively level ground to a grassy section along the river at 0.7 mile. This is a good location for an easy backpack. If you walk to the river's bank, you will get a close-up view of the confluence of Warm Springs Creek and the South Fork of the Payette River. (See hike 29 to experience Warm Springs Creek.)

Beyond the confluence, the trail crosses a talus slide area and soon arrives at another level area near the river at 1.1 miles. This would also be a good backpack destination. Continue east passing a spring at 1.4 miles and then over a large, unnamed creek at 1.8 miles. The trail now rises nearly 100 feet, and the forest is a bit more open with smaller conifers and a few aspen. At 2.4 miles, reach an unsigned, faint junction. Continue east on the foot trail, and make a circle back to the unsigned junction within 500 feet. Retrace your steps 2.4 miles back to the trailhead.

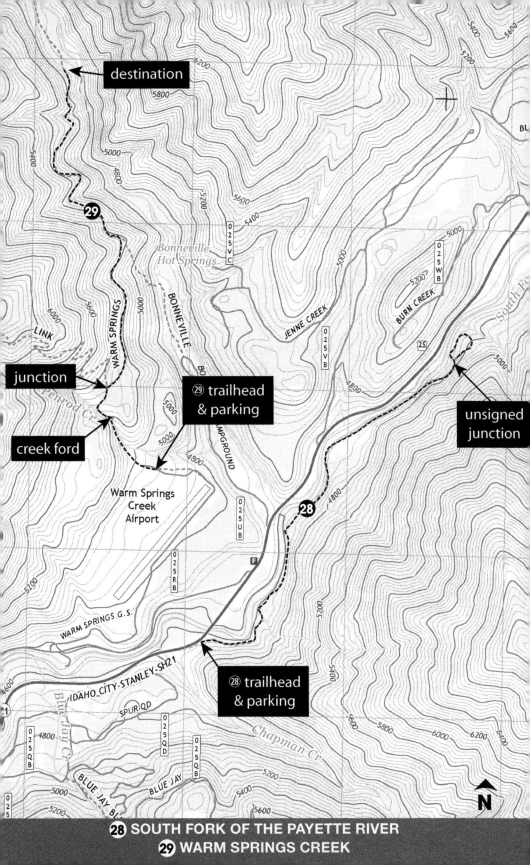

destination

29

Bonneville
Hot Springs

025VC

025WB

5200

BURN CREEK

JENNE CREEK

025VB

25

5000

unsigned
junction

WARM SPRINGS

BONNEVILLE

LINK

junction

29 trailhead
& parking

creek ford

Warm Springs
Creek
Airport

025UB

025RB

28

South Fork

WARM SPRINGS G.S.

IDAHO CITY-STANLEY-SH21

SPUR QD

28 trailhead
& parking

025QD

025QB

Chapman Cr

BLUE JAY CR

025QB

025QB

BLUE JAY BL

BLUE JAY

025

N

28 SOUTH FORK OF THE PAYETTE RIVER
29 WARM SPRINGS CREEK

29 WARM SPRINGS CREEK

Coordinates

Trailhead
N 44° 08.751'
W 115° 18.653'
Warm Springs Creek
N 44° 10.077'
W 115° 19.275'

Distance: 4.6 miles out-and-back
Total Elevation Gain: 800 feet
Difficulty: 🚶🚶🚶
Elevation Range: 4,950 to 5,200 feet
Topographic Map: Jackson Peak
Time: 2.5 to 3 hours
Season: Mid-April through early November
Water Availability: Warm Springs Creek, many tributary streams
Cautionary Advice: None
Additional Information: Boise National Forest, Lowman Ranger District (208) 365-7000
Pit Latrine: No

WARM SPRINGS CREEK

Mid-to-late springtime along Warm Springs Creek is a chance to lose yourself in a wilderness of thick old-growth forest, blooming wildflowers and the beautiful Warm Springs Creek. Melting snow transforms the normally serene creek into a turbulent waterway that twists through a picturesque canyon gorge on its way to a confluence with the South Fork of the Payette River. Pockets of Douglas fir and lodgepole and ponderosa pine are sprinkled along the steep slopes. It's no mystery why this may be the most stunning hike near Lowman.

Most of this outing is along steep hillsides, at times nearly 500 feet above Warm Springs Creek. As you make your way north, the views looking to the west-facing canyon wall above the creek are exceptional. The trail eventually descends to the canyon floor where a bubbling hot spring oozes creekside. Ponderosa pines and a lush understory invite an overnight stay.

The hike can be extended because the trail continues beyond this point. The trail is fairly level as it meanders along the canyon floor weaving under old-growth forest. There are many hillside meadows with a profusion of spring wildflowers, and there is a bounty of spots to camp. Because of the trail's low elevation and southern exposure, this is a great destination after mid-April when the forest road to the trailhead is open. The valley floor is an excellent place to see deer, elk and black bear, and mountain goats are often seen on the canyon cliffs.

DRIVING DIRECTIONS

From the junction of the Banks-Lowman Highway and ID 21, drive east on ID 21 for 18.3 miles. Turn left on dirt-surfaced FR 025RC. There will be a sign for the Warm Springs Creek Trailhead. Follow FR 025RC for 0.9 mile, and turn right on FR 025RB at the Warm Springs Guard Station. Follow this road for 1.4 miles as it winds around the Warm Springs landing strip to its end at the signed trailhead.

If you continue east on ID 21 past FR 025RC, you will come to a short forest road leading north that provides access to the beautiful Bonneville Campground. From the campground, you can hike a quarter-mile to Bonneville Hot Springs.

Grassy meadow near the Warm Springs Creek trailhead

Old-growth forest

THE HIKE

From the trailhead, cross a grassy meadow and enter forest. Ford the shallow Penrod Creek at 0.3 mile as the trail rises nearly 100 feet to a junction at 0.5 mile. (The left fork begins a very steep ascent to the 7,871-foot Eightmile Mountain.) Continue along the right fork as you wander through dense old-growth forest and then onto an open hillside perched high above Bonneville Hot Springs. In spring, arrowleaf balsamroot is copious along this stretch.

At 1.0 mile, reenter forest as the trail stays fairly level and crosses a ravine at 1.6 miles. The views from the hillside are exceptional looking to the east and down to Warm Springs Creek. Ascend nearly 100 feet from the ravine and then descend to a small, unnamed creek. At 2.3 miles, the trail finally levels beside Warm Springs Creek. There is a good campsite here, and a small footpath leads to a creekside hot springs. This is the destination.

If you want to extend the hike, the trail continues north along the west side of Warm Springs Creek. There is only modest elevation gain through open hillsides and old-growth forest. There are many places to camp. At 6.7 miles, there is a bridge over Warm Springs Creek. From the bridge, the hiking is much more rigorous, and the trail continues another 7.7 miles to Bull Trout Lake.

Warm Springs Creek

30 WEST MOUNTAIN TRAIL

Coordinates

Trailhead
N 44° 19.399'
W 116° 08.849'

Hilltop Meadow
N 44° 20.856'
W 116° 08.101'

Distance: 4.3 miles out-and-back
Total Elevation Gain: 900 feet
Difficulty: 🏃🏃🏃
Elevation Range: 6,100 to 6,800 feet
Topographic Map: Sagehen Reservoir
Time: 2.5 to 3 hours
Season: Late June through October
Water Availability: Several creeks
Cautionary Advice: Expect grazing cattle
Additional Information: Boise National Forest, Emmett Ranger District (208) 365-7000
Pit Latrine: No

WEST MOUNTAIN TRAIL

The West Mountain Trail has plenty to like: lush forest, wildflower-covered hillsides, ambling creeks and wonderful vistas. The singletrack trail begins just north of FR 626 and meanders through old-growth forest for about a mile. There are several small creeks, and the forest floor is covered with ferns and many other plants.

The second mile is a bit different as you gain elevation along hillsides often with open forest of Douglas firs and close-packed aspen. In early October, this is a good hike for fall color. The hike destination is a broad hilltop meadow that delivers outstanding views north to the 8,082-foot Tripod Peak. Nearby, several granite outcroppings offer fine perches to enjoy the views. There are also many large Douglas firs, and the wildflowers are abundant in early summer, especially cinquefoil and horsemint.

This hike is rarely level although most of the trail's grades are moderate. There are grazing cattle in the area, so it is possible you will see a few near the higher elevations of the hike. The hike can be extended beyond the hilltop meadow, but it becomes much more strenuous.

DRIVING DIRECTIONS

From the junction of ID 55 and State Street in Boise, drive north on ID 55 for 52.1 miles to Smith's Ferry and look for a sign on the right side of the road ("Sportsman Access Tripod Res."). Turn left (west) onto the dirt-surfaced FR 644, and proceed 2.0 miles to a signed junction. Reset your tripmeter, and turn right on FR 626. Follow the sign to Sagehen Reservoir. Continue 4.1 miles on FR 626 to a spur road marked "Trail 311" on the right (north). You may park here or follow the spur road 0.1 mile to the trailhead.

THE HIKE

From the parking area at the end of the spur road, head north about 75 yards and then veer right (east) on a singletrack trail. There will be an information board to the right of the trailhead, signed "131." The trail enters dense forest with Engelmann spruce and lodgepole pine. After a descent of 150 feet in 0.3 mile, cross a tiny stream. Begin a modest ascent, cross another stream at 0.4 mile and then make two easy fords of a shallow, unnamed creek at 0.7 mile.

Beyond the second creek ford, the trail's grade intensifies and leaves the forest behind. After a gain of more than 100 feet, the trail levels at 1.0 mile in open forest. The route starts a modest rise again as it passes through patches of forest and along open hillsides. Aspen is prolific along this section.

The trail temporarily levels again at 1.5 miles and makes a short descent, passing a huge Douglas fir tree at 1.7 miles. From here, continue through a dense stand of aspen, and make a final gain of 150 feet to an open meadow at 2.1 miles. Near the end of the hilltop meadow is a small granite outcropping to the west (left) of the trail. This is the end of the hike. There are several outcroppings east and west of the trail that offer nice platforms to enjoy a snack and observe the wonderful views. Looking directly north, you can see Tripod Peak and the active fire lookout on its apex. Another great vista is to walk to the west side of the meadow and look southwest into Ola Valley.

If you want to extend the hike from the meadow, the trail descends 250 feet over the next half-mile before rising to 6,700 feet and an unsigned junction in a little meadow at 4.4 miles. You can turn left (west) here and continue another 1.9 miles with more than 1,300 feet of gain to the top of Tripod Mountain.

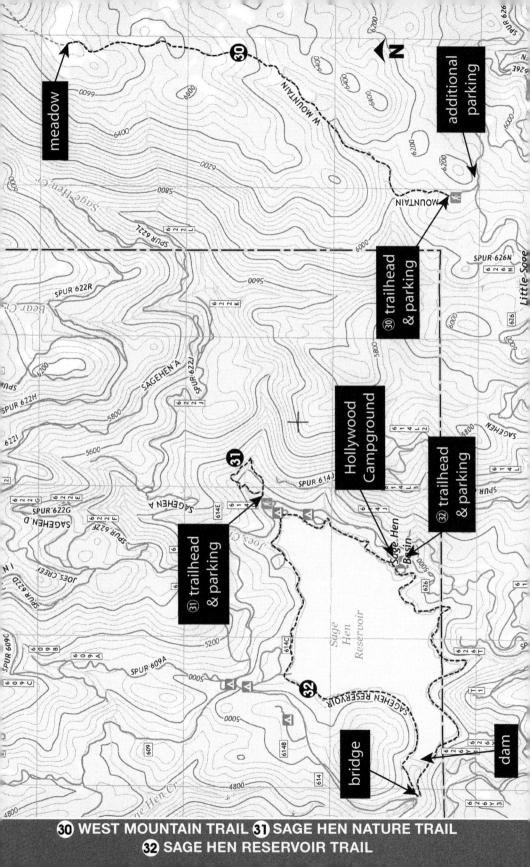

30 WEST MOUNTAIN TRAIL 31 SAGE HEN NATURE TRAIL
32 SAGE HEN RESERVOIR TRAIL

Coordinates

Trailhead

N 44° 20.143'

W 116° 10.372'

First Waterfall

N 44° 20.162'

W 116° 10.220'

Distance: 0.5 mile loop

Total Elevation Gain: 100 feet

Difficulty: 🧍

Elevation Range: 5,000 to 5,100 feet

Topographic Map: Sage Hen Reservoir

Time: 30 minutes

Season: Late May through early November

Water Availability: Several creeks

Cautionary Advice: None

Additional Information: Boise National Forest, Emmett Ranger District (208) 365-7000

Pit Latrine: No

SAGE HEN NATURE TRAIL

With its lush forest of Engelmann spruce, grand fir and lodgepole pine, cascading waterfalls and boulder-lined trail, the Sage Hen Nature trail packs a lot of scenic beauty for a short, loop hike. Starting from the east side of Sage Hen Reservoir near the Sage Hen and Eastside campgrounds, the pedestrian-only trail parallels Sage Hen Creek while crossing several little, wooden bridges. It soon arrives at a wide, 12-foot high waterfall spilling into a boulder-lined pool.

A footpath heads upstream about 250 feet to yet another waterfall. There are several huge boulders and a wide-canopied forest—the perfect place for a serene picnic. From the two waterfalls, the trail loops back to the trailhead through forest and over a couple of tiny streams. Along the route, there are several well-positioned wooden benches that allow you to take a contemplative moment and enjoy this little sanctuary.

DRIVING DIRECTIONS

From State Street and ID 55, travel north on ID 55 for 19.7 miles to

Horseshoe Bend. Turn left (west) on State Highway 52. Continue 9.1 miles to the Sweet-Ola Highway, then turn right. Reset your tripmeter, and continue through the small town of Ola at 16 miles. Continue north to a junction with FR 626 at 27.4 miles. (The road becomes FR 618 and turns to a dirt surface at 19.5 miles.) Turn right on FR 626, and continue 5.9 miles. Turn left on FR 614. Continue on FR 614 for 3.4 miles to the signed trailhead on the left side of the road.

An alternate route to the Sage Hen area—about the same amount of driving time— is via FR 626 from Smith's Ferry. Be advised that FR 626 is narrow and very curvy.

Sage Hen Creek

THE HIKE

The hike is described counterclockwise, which will take you to the most scenic area of the hike first. From the trailhead, head into forest and then cross a bridge within 250 feet. The trail turns upstream and comes to another bridge below the large waterfall. There is a bench just beyond the bridge.

A few yards past the waterfall at 0.2 mile, a user-created trail continues upstream about 75 feet, weaving between large rocks to another waterfall. Although the footpath continues beyond the waterfall and is cut into the side of the canyon, it is very steep and has difficult footing in some sections.

To continue to the trailhead, at the junction with the footpath continue on the main trail as it turns west through lush, dense forest. Before crossing a bridge over a small stream, you will find another wooden bench. The trail crosses one last bridge at 0.4 mile. Soon after, you will reach the trailhead.

Coordinates

Trailhead

  N 44° 19.593'
  W 116° 10.697'

Dam

  N 44° 19.515'
  W 116° 11.688'

Distance: 4.2 miles loop
Total Elevation Gain: 400 feet
Difficulty: 🚶🚶🚶
Elevation Range: 4,900 to 5,000 feet
Topographic Map: Sage Hen Reservoir
Time: 2.5 hours
Season: Mid-May through early November
Water Availability: Sage Hen Reservoir, several creeks
Cautionary Advice: None
Additional Information: Boise National Forest, Emmett Ranger District (208) 365-7000
Pit Latrine: At the Hollywood Campground

SAGE HEN RESERVOIR TRAIL

The Sage Hen Reservoir is located along the western perimeter of the Boise National Forest southwest of Cascade Lake. The circular-shaped reservoir is surrounded by a close-packed forest of Engelman spruce, ponderosa and lodgepole pine, and Douglas and grand firs. There are five campgrounds strewn around the lake; most are on its east and north sides. The lake is stocked with rainbow trout, and there are good opportunities to see wildlife in the area.

The Sage Hen Reservoir trail circumnavigates the lake and is fairly level the entire route. There are a multitude of trailheads because the trail wanders through or near all the campgrounds. By far, the most scenic section of the hike is to start from the Hollywood Campground, and head west to the primitive dam. (There is free trailhead parking before entering the campground.) Since there are no campgrounds along this section of the lake, you experience a genuine feeling of wilderness.

The singletrack trail winds through several beautiful side drainages with bridged streams. At 1.5 miles (near the dam), you reach the southwest corner of the lake where there is a outcropping to enjoy the scenery. You could turn around here for a wonderful three mile out-and-back hike. If you continue beyond the dam, the scenery is still pleasant. However, the forest is more open, the trail is often an old road and you hike through campgrounds. This detracts a little from the secluded experience. Whether you hike to the dam or around the lake, it is a worthy outing. Another suggestion is to start from the Sagehen Dam picnic area, and hike east to the Hollywood Campground.

DRIVING DIRECTIONS

From State Street and ID 55, travel north on ID 55 for 19.7 miles to Horseshoe Bend. Turn left (west) on State Highway 52. Continue 9.1 miles to the Sweet-Ola Highway and then turn right. Reset your tripmeter, and continue through the small town of Ola at 16 miles. Continue north to a junction with FR 626 at 27.4 miles. (The

Dense forest surrounds Sage Hen Reservoir

road becomes FR 618 and turns to a dirt surface at 19.5 miles.) Turn right on FR 626, and continue 5.9 miles. Turn left on FR 614. Continue on FR 614 for 4.1 miles to a parking area (west side of the road) just before entering the Hollywood Campground.

An alternate route to the Sage Hen area—about the same amount of driving time—is via FR 626 from Smith's Ferry. Be advised that FR 626 is narrow and very curvy.

THE HIKE

The trail is described clockwise, which enables you to see the most scenic section of the hike first and allows you to turnaround at the dam to shorten the hiking distance. From the parking area, look for the singletrack trail on its left side (southwest). Descend through forest about 20 yards and then turn left (south) at a junction. Cross a small bridge as the trail turns west.

At a quarter-mile, you will come to a sandy beach—a nice destination. A side trail turns to the left—do not take this trail. Continue straight. The trail turns south up a "finger" of the lake and crosses a bridge over a small stream at 0.5 mile. The woods are dense and beautiful. Beyond the bridge, gain about 50 feet of elevation and descend to another bridge at 0.9 mile. Just beyond the bridge, look for a huge granite boulder perched on the edge of the lake.

Continue along the perimeter of the lake, then ford a small stream at 1.4 miles. The trail then rises over a little rocky knoll and descends to a outcropping at 1.5 miles. This is a great destination, just feet from the rocky dam.

To continue around the lake, walk past the dam and then cross a bridge over Sage Hen Creek at 1.7 miles near the Sage Hen picnic area. There are tables and beautiful forest—another good stop. Turn right, and head east on the wide trail. Most of the hike beyond this point is along an old roadbed, so you lose a little of the intimate feeling of the wooded singletrack. At 1.8 miles, there is an unsigned junction. Stay left and ascend 75 feet. At the top of the climb, a side trail veers right to a beach area.

Continue north through dense forest. Eventually the trail turns east across a paved parking lot at 2.7 miles; this is the Antelope Campground and boat launch. Continue along the north side of the lake passing below some enormous ponderosa pines. At 2.9 miles the trail returns to a singletrack and enters the Sage Hen Campground at 3.2 miles. Continue along the paved road, passing Joe's Creek and then Sage Hen Creek.

The route then turns south and returns to a singletrack once again. Pass on the backside of the Eastside Campground at 3.8 miles. The trail wanders through forest, across a couple of streams and comes to an unsigned junction at 4.1 miles. This is the perimeter of the Hollywood Campground. To return to the trailhead, the shortest route is to turn left and reach the trailhead in 600 feet. If you continue straight at the unsigned junction, the trail leads past the perimeter of the campground and soon arrives at the junction where you started the hike near the trailhead.

33 MACKS CREEK

Coordinates

Trailhead

N 43° 36.584'
W 115° 55.932'

End of Hike

N 43° 37.543'
W 115° 56.538'

Distance: 3.0 miles out-and-back
Total Elevation Gain: 400 feet
Difficulty: 🚶🚶
Elevation Range: 3,100 to 3,500 feet
Topographic Map: Arrowrock Dam
Time: 1.5 hours
Season: All year
Water Availability: Macks Creek (seasonal)
Cautionary Advice: None
Additional Information: Boise National Forest, Mountain Home Ranger District (208) 587-7961
Pit Latrine: No. There is one at Macks Creek Park before reaching the trailhead.

MACKS CREEK

Between Lucky Peak Lake and Arrowrock Reservoir is a little-known hike that parallels Macks Creek. The singletrack trail meanders along a modest grade up a broad drainage, occasionally passing below hillside outcroppings. The area is a riparian habitat. In spring, listen for songbirds, including wrens, finches, warblers and mountain bluebirds (the state bird of Idaho). Macks Creek is lined with cottonwood trees, willows, alder and other shrubs—fine perches for songbirds.

Look along the open hillsides surrounding the drainage for elk and mule deer in winter and spring. The best time to experience the area is late April, May and early June. The treeless hillsides are green, wildflowers bloom and the flora-lined creek comes to life. The trailhead is about a quarter-mile east of Macks Creek Park, a recreational site with picnic benches, sandy beaches, a boat launch and RV and tent camping sites.

Rush skeletonweed is prevalent along the drainage bottom. This perennial plant—considered a noxious weed—produces a bright yellow flower in late spring and early summer. The weed is common in the Boise foothills and is edible for sheep and goats.

Macks Creek is fun to explore after a winter snow

DRIVING DIRECTIONS

From the intersection of Warm Springs Avenue and ID 21, drive north on ID 21 for 9.3 miles. After crossing the Mores Creek Bridge, turn right onto the paved FR 268. Proceed 4.9 miles—passing through Macks Creek Park where there is a pit latrine—to the unmarked trailhead on your left (north). There is parking on both sides of the road.

THE HIKE

Walk north along the dirt road about 500 feet to a sign indicating no motorized travel. The singletrack trail continues north and veers northwest at 0.4 mile, below dark gray outcroppings. The route crosses a wide spot in the canyon where the invasive rush skeletonweed is prolific. This perennial plant competes for water and nitrogen with native species and has become a problem in the Pacific Northwest, especially in Idaho.

Cross an intermittent stream at 1.3 miles, which may have water in spring. At 1.5 miles, the trail fades at the end of the drainage. Look to the left for a footpath that leads to a stand of trees—a worthy destination for

a picnic. Here too a couple of steep ravines, one to the west and one leading north, offer interesting off-trail explorations. Deer and elk are usually seen in the evenings.

Macks Creek drainage

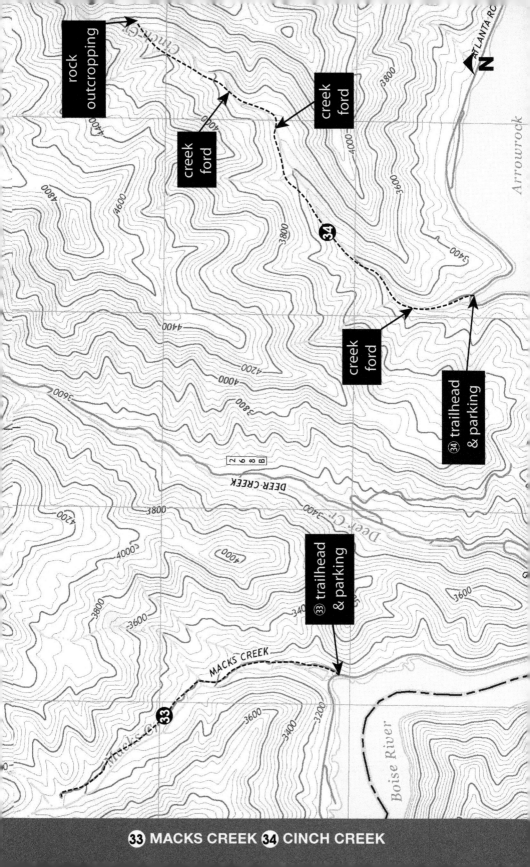

rock outcropping

creek ford

creek ford

34

creek ford

34 trailhead & parking

DEER CREEK

B 8 6 2

Deer Cr. 3400

33 trailhead & parking

MACKS CREEK

Macks Cr.

33

Boise River

ATLANTA RD

Arrowrock

N

33 MACKS CREEK 34 CINCH CREEK

34 CINCH CREEK

Distance: 3.4 miles out-and-back
Total Elevation Gain: 950 feet
Difficulty: 🚶🚶🚶
Elevation Range: 3,250 to 4,100 feet
Topographic Map: Arrowrock Dam
Time: 2 hours
Season: All year
Water Availability: Cinch Creek
Cautionary Advice: None
Additional Information: Be aware of hunters in fall.
Pit Latrine: No

Coordinates
Trailhead
N 43° 36.202'
W 115° 54.501'
Rock Outcropping
N 43° 37.168'
W 115° 53.420'

CINCH CREEK

Cinch Creek invites seekers of solitude. Though it snakes through a scenic setting among the steep hills north of popular Arrowrock Reservoir, it appears only a few folks know about this primitive trail.

The narrow foot trail begins a few yards from FR 268 near the edge of Arrowrock Reservoir and meanders north. After an easy ford of Cinch Creek, it turns east and has a somewhat vigorous 250-foot rise that parallels Cinch Creek. Beyond this point, the trail has a modest grade.

Steep hillsides with sagebrush and an occasional ponderosa pine frame the route. There are several choice locations to stop for a secluded picnic, including a couple of the easy fords of Cinch Creek and a hillside outcropping at the end of the hike description. The low elevation of the area ensures year-round hiking, although summer can be very hot. Spring is probably the best time to hike with fall being a close second because of the October foliage. Think twice during hunting season though because this is prime elk and deer habitat.

Cinch Creek drainage

DRIVING DIRECTIONS

From the intersection of Warm Springs Avenue and ID 21 on the east side of Boise, drive north 9.3 miles on ID 21. Turn right onto the paved FR 268 towards Atlanta. Reset your tripmeter. Continue 8.1 miles. (The road turns to a dirt-surfaced road at 5.3 miles.) You will find a small parking area on the left side (north) of FR 268. There is parking for two or three vehicles.

THE HIKE

From the parking area, head north with a rock-hop ford of Cinch Creek at 0.1 mile. The trail turns east and begins the most strenuous part of the hike. Cross a tiny stream at 0.3 mile, and bypass a outcropping at 0.4 mile. At 0.5 mile, the trail levels, having gained 250 feet from the ford of Cinch Creek.

The trail now winds through a little side drainage and enters a level area where the canyon is wider. At 1.0 mile and 1.3 miles, ford Cinch Creek. The second ford is lined with willows and cottonwoods, providing a shaded respite. Continue northeast along a modest grade passing to the south of a large outcropping at 1.4 miles. Beyond here, the trail dips through a little ravine and enters an area with lots of sagebrush then fades away.

If you look to your right (south), a faint footpath descends to the cottonwood-lined Cinch Creek. You can ford the creek here and continue about 500 feet to a large outcropping perched above the drainage with very good views both up and down the canyon. (You must ascend about 75 feet.)

35 COTTONWOOD CREEK

Coordinates

Trailhead
N 43° 39.557'
W 115° 50.112'
**Destination beyond
the last Bridge**
N 43° 40.732'
W 115° 49.246'

Distance: 3.6 miles out-and-back
Total Elevation Gain: 650 feet
Difficulty: 🚶🚶🚶
Elevation Range: 3,700 to 4,350 feet
Topographic Map: Arrowrock Reservoir Northeast, Twin Springs
Time: 2 hours
Season: April through November
Water Availability: Cottonwood Creek
Cautionary Advice: Watch for rattlesnakes during the summer months.
Additional Information: Boise National Forest, Mountain Home Ranger District (208) 587-7961
Pit Latrine: No

COTTONWOOD CREEK

In July of 1994, a lightning strike caused the massive Rabbit Creek Fire that burned nearly 150,000 acres in the Boise National Forest. The fire was extinguished after seventy-three days by fall rains and snow. The high-intensity fire burned in the Cottonwood Creek drainage and badly burned the flora along the steep slopes.

A spring hike along Cottonwood Creek is a great introduction to forest recovery years after a major burn because saplings and bushes are retaking the landscape. Within the first mile of the hike, signs of the devastating fire are apparent, and trees become scarcer the higher you ascend. However, the lack of trees allows many wildflowers to grow, including spring beauty, sego lily, yarrow, scarlet gila, stonecrop, clarika, cinquefoil, forget-me-not, larkspur, sulphur flower, monkey flower, threadleaf phacelia and false hellebore.

Cottonwood Creek is a major tributary of the North Fork of the Boise River and is bordered by dogwood, alder, birch and ferns. There are a few stands of beautiful ponderosa pines that survived the fire and provide pleasant destinations for a backpack trip. In fact, the destination for this hike is a charming setting along Cottonwood Creek where a large stand of huge ponderosa pines thrive. After the wildflowers expire, usually by late June, look to hike in the fall when aspen, shrubs and other plants provide autumn colors. Midsummer hiking can be extremely hot in the canyon.

DRIVING DIRECTIONS

From the intersection of Warm Springs Avenue and ID 21, drive north in ID for 9.3 miles. Turn right onto paved FR 268. Drive 15.6 miles. (The road turns to a dirt-surface at 5.3 miles.) Turn left on FR 377. Drive 2.3 miles to the signed trailhead on the right.

The Cottonwood Campground (three sites along Cottonwood Creek) is located 1.7 miles before reaching the trailhead on FR 377. Near the trailhead, dispersed camping is available along Cottonwood Creek.

THE HIKE

From the signed trail-head, ascend under a canopy of old-growth forest, mostly pon-derosa pine. After a gain of 300 feet, the trail levels at 0.7 mile. Evidence of the fire is very apparent; most of the old-growth trees are burned. At 1.0 mile, cross Cot-tonwood Creek on a wooden bridge. Stay

Bridge near Cottonwood Creek destination

on the north side of the creek for a quarter-mile and then cross another bridge over Cottonwood Creek at 1.3 miles. About 500 feet beyond the bridge, pass a few large ponderosa pines and level terrain, which makes for good camping.

Cross the creek again to its north side on one last bridge at 1.7 miles.

The trail now turns east under a large stand of ponderosa pines. The ground is level and the setting quite scenic. The nearby terrain is worthy of off-trail exploration. This is your destination.

If you want to extend the hike, you can continue up the trail along Cottonwood Creek. Most of the trees in the canyon are burned beyond this point, so don't expect a lot of shade. However, if you hike in spring, you are compensated with an array of beautiful wildflowers. You will immediately gain 200 feet and come to a ford of Cottonwood Creek—no more bridges—at 2.4 miles.

The trail continues to gradually rise crossing Cottonwood Creek twice at 3.4 miles. At 4.0 miles, enter a broad sagebrush-covered meadow—elevation 4,900 feet—where Sawmill Creek confluences with Cottonwood Creek. Backpackers will find camping opportunities on the opposite side of Cottonwood Creek near Sawmill Creek.

Northeast view in Cottonwood Creek drainage

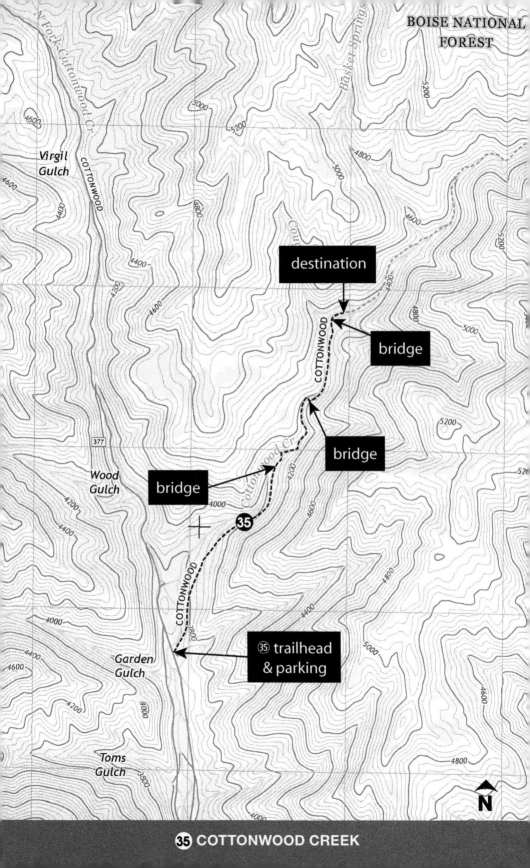

BOISE NATIONAL
FOREST

N. Fork Cottonwood Cr.

Virgil
Gulch

COTTONWOOD

Basket Springs

5200

5000

5200

4600

4800

5000

4600

destination

bridge

COTTONWOOD

4800

5000

377

Wood
Gulch

bridge

4200

Cottonwood Cr.

bridge

5200

52

35

Cottonwood Cr.

4000

COTTONWOOD

4800

Garden
Gulch

35 trailhead
& parking

5000

4600

Toms
Gulch

N

35 COTTONWOOD CREEK

36 SADDLE ABOVE LOGGING GULCH

Coordinates

Trailhead
N 43° 40.963'
W 115° 40.657'

Saddle
N 43° 41.593'
W 115° 40.600'

Distance: 1.8 miles out-and-back
Total Elevation Gain: 500 feet
Difficulty:
Elevation Range: 3,400 to 3,900 feet
Topographic Map: Twin Springs
Time: 1.5 hours
Season: All year
Water Availability: None
Cautionary Advice: Watch for rattlesnakes in summer.
Additional Information: Boise National Forest, Mountain Home Ranger District (208) 634-0400
Pit Latrine: No

SADDLE ABOVE LOGGING GULCH

Thomas Jefferson once quipped, "The best thinking has been done in solitude." If this little witticism rings true for you, you might just catch an inspirational thought on this short hike. You can be assured that solitude will be a constant on this unknown outing.

The hike begins feet from the Middle Fork of the Boise River along an old dirt road that is closed to motorized use. It passes through open terrain scattered with sagebrush and small outcroppings. Ahead lies a furrowed landscape of rolling hills and mountains. The final segment of the hike meanders up a hillside strewn with old-growth pine trees. The destination (just west of Logging Gulch) is a 3,900-foot saddle covered with pine needles and a stand of trees. It is a beautiful setting.

If you have the stamina, you can veer south off-trail and ascend 200 feet along a rolling ridge. In less than a quarter-mile, you will reach the lofty perch of a treeless 4,109-foot hilltop. The views from here are spectacular. Looking east, and nearly 1,000 feet below, is the Middle Fork of the Boise River as it snakes through the deep canyon below. Looking southeast, Sheep Mountain rises high above the cliff-lined river. To the north, forested mountains unfurl ridge over ridge.

DRIVING DIRECTIONS

From the intersection of Warm Springs Avenue and ID 21, drive north on ID 21 for 9.3 miles. Turn right onto the paved FR 268 towards Atlanta. Reset your tripmeter, and continue a winding 28.0 miles to an unsigned parking area on the left (north) side of the road. (The road turns into a dirt-surface at 5.3 miles.) If you come to the bridge over the Middle Fork of the Boise River on FR 268, you have gone too far. There is a short spur road just prior to the parking area that leads to a dispersed campsite.

THE HIKE

From the parking area, walk up the dirt road a few yards to a signpost. (It was laying on the ground at last visit.) Just past the trailhead, the ground has been razed to stop motorized use, so look closely for the trail. The footpath veers right, and soon the old road becomes apparent. Continue north paralleling a ravine lined with cottonwood trees. Looking west, several outcroppings dot the open landscape. At 0.5 mile, the route nears the base of the hills ahead, and within 500 feet enters an area with very large sagebrush.

At 0.7 mile, the road veers right (east) and fades at the ravine—it will likely have water in the spring. Cross the ravine and then veer south on a pine-needle-covered old roadbed. After a modest ascent, reach the flat, tree-covered saddle at 0.9 mile. This is a wonderful destination to enjoy a picnic or just relish the solitude.

From the saddle, the trail turns north and descends 200 feet in 0.3 mile to where it is nearly impossible to proceed due to dense vegetation. If you walk down the route the first 500 feet though, there are good views looking down to the Logging Gulch drainage. A better option to extend the hike from the saddle is to veer right up an open hillside. (See map.) After a gain of nearly 200 feet in 0.2 mile, you will reach a flat hilltop offering exceptional vistas. There are steep drop-offs to the south of the hill, so this added extension is not recommended for children.

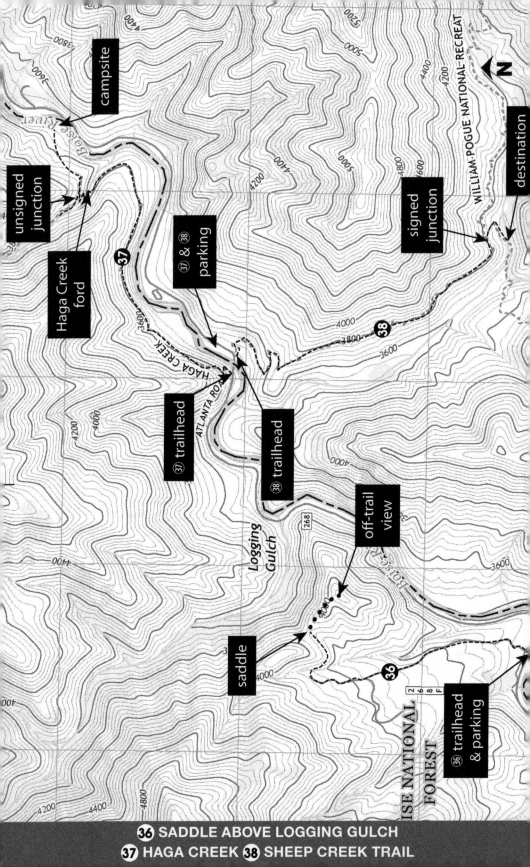

campsite

unsigned junction

Haga Creek ford

37

37 & 38 parking

HAGA CREEK

ATLANTA ROAD

37 trailhead

38 trailhead

Logging Gulch

268

off-trail view

saddle

Boise River

WILLIAM-POGUE NATIONAL-RECREAT

destination

signed junction

38

Boise River

N

36

36 trailhead & parking

BOISE NATIONAL FOREST

36 SADDLE ABOVE LOGGING GULCH
37 HAGA CREEK 38 SHEEP CREEK TRAIL

37 HAGA CREEK

Coordinates

Trailhead
N 43° 41.808'
W 115° 39.573'

Haga Creek Ford
N 43° 42.242'
W 115° 38.856'

Distance: 2.5 miles out-and-back
Total Elevation Gain: 500 feet
Difficulty: 🚶🚶
Elevation Range: 3,450 to 3,650 feet
Topographic Map: Twin Springs
Time: 1.5 hours
Season: All year
Water Availability: Middle Fork of the Boise River, Haga Creek
Cautionary Advice: There are a couple of short segments along the trail with steep drop-offs, so the hike is not advised for small children.
Additional Information: Boise National Forest, Mountain Home Ranger District (208) 587-7961
Pit Latrine: No

HAGA CREEK

If you have not discovered this seldom-traveled trail, you will likely be surprised by the beauty this outing offers. The journey starts with a 150-foot, switch-backed ascent up a steep hillside that is the most strenuous segment of the hike. It soon levels and provides outstanding vistas up and down the crystalline waters of the Middle Fork of the Boise River. From here, the trail—cut high into hillside above the river's north bank—parallels the river for nearly a mile.

The trail eventually turns north at the confluence of Haga Creek with the Middle Fork of the Boise River. You can venture off trail about 500 feet to a level area set under a canopy of lofty ponderosa pines along the river's edge—a perfect location for a contemplative break or backpack. If you continue north, the trail crosses the tree-lined Haga Creek, which is the end of the hike. You can extend the hike with a couple of options either along the Middle Fork of the Boise River or up the Haga Creek drainage.

Because of the area's low elevation, the hike is accessible year-round ex-

View southwest near the trailhead

cept after a heavy snow. Arguably, the best time to experience the area is late April and early May when the open hillsides above Haga Creek explode in an outrageous show of yellow. Here, the yellow-flowering arrowleaf balsamroot grows thick on the steep hillsides. If you time your hike for the flower's peak bloom, you will likely return the following spring.

DRIVING DIRECTIONS

From the intersection of Warm Springs Avenue and ID 21 on the east side of Boise, drive north on ID 21 for 9.3 miles. Turn right onto the paved FR 268 towards Atlanta. Reset your tripmeter. Wind 29.7 miles. (The road turns into a dirt-surface at 5.3 miles.) The signed trailhead is on the left side of the road, just before the bridge over the Middle Fork of the Boise River. Although there is a pullout for a single vehicle on the south side of the road, it is best to follow FR 268 over the bridge to a large parking area for the Sheep Creek Trail on the north side of the road. (See hike 38.)

THE HIKE

From the signed trailhead, ascend through two switchbacks as the trail temporarily levels at 0.2 mile. The views from this perch are outstanding. Make a gentle descent of 100 feet to an easy ford of a tiny stream at 0.4 mile.

From here, ascend

View west from the Haga Creek Trail

about 50 feet as the trail undulates over the next half-mile along the sloped hills above the river. At 1.0 mile, just before the trail turns north away from the Middle Fork of the Boise River, you can venture off-trail and descend 100 feet to the river's bank where you will find ponderosa pines, mine tailings and a level area where you could certainly establish an easy backpack.

If you are hiking in midspring, you will see many blooming arrowleaf balsamroot once you turn up the Haga Creek drainage. The trail soon comes to Haga Creek, which you will ford at 1.25 miles. If you want to extend the hike, ford the narrow Haga Creek, then ascend through three switchbacks to an unsigned junction at 1.5 miles. If you turn right (east), the foot trail descends about 200 feet in a quarter-mile to a level area with ponderosa pines along the Middle Fork's bank. You could establish a campsite here too. The only negative is that FR 268 is on the other side of the river, so you will occasionally hear vehicle traffic.

Another option at the unsigned junction is to continue north on the main trail alongside Haga Creek. The trail is fairly level for a half-mile and soon comes within feet of Haga Creek near a few outcroppings. This area is a good turnaround location. Beyond it, the trail's grade is much steeper as it parallels Haga Creek. There are many scenic outcroppings, occasional dense forest and great over-the-shoulder views as you move higher. As you make your way north, you will find good backpack destinations at 2.9 and 3.1 miles.

Outcroppings along Haga Creek

38 SHEEP CREEK TRAIL

Coordinates

Trailhead
N 43° 41.800'
W 115° 39.493'

Sheep Creek
N 43° 41.019'
W 115° 39.002'

Distance: 3.0 miles out-and-back
Total Elevation Gain: 600 feet
Difficulty: 🚶🚶🚶
Elevation Range: 3,450 to 3,850 feet
Topographic Map: Sheep Creek
Time: 1.5 to 2 hours
Season: March through early December
Water Availability: Sheep Creek
Cautionary Advice: Watch for rattlesnakes during the summer months.
Additional Information: Boise National Forest, Mountain Home Ranger District (208) 587-7961
Pit Latrine: No

SHEEP CREEK TRAIL

Sheep Creek Trail exemplifies everything that is wonderful about hiking near the Middle Fork of the Boise River: nearly year-round access, beautiful old-growth ponderosa pines, spectacular fall and spring foliage, a pristine creek, beautiful outcroppings and plenty of solitude. This superb hike starts near the confluence of Sheep Creek with the Middle Fork of the Boise River. It then heads south along a rocky hillside delivering spectacular vistas of this often-overlooked area.

The destination in a dense stand of old-growth ponderosa pines is along the banks of Sheep Creek. Here you can establish an easy backpack camp or enjoy a serene break. There is plenty of shade and a slew of oversized boulders lining the creek. Sheep Creek is substantial. In spring, you might guess it's a river. The area has plenty of wildlife including deer, elk, coyotes and black bears. Raptors such as eagles and hawks often soar over the deep drainage, too.

If you are looking to camp near the trailhead, there are several excellent dispersed campsites along the Middle Fork of the Boise River both before and after the trailhead. The Troutdale Campground is just a few miles east of the trailhead. An added bonus to this hike is that to the right of the Sheep Creek trailhead is a short foot-path leading to the Sheep Creek Hot Springs, perched above the Middle Fork of the Boise River. You can also hike nearby Haga Creek trail too. (See hike 37.)

DRIVING DIRECTIONS

From the junction of Warm Springs Avenue and ID 21, drive northeast 9.3 miles on ID 21 and across the Mores Creek Bridge. Make an immediate right (east) onto the paved FR 268. Reset

Sheep Creek in April

your tripmeter and then drive a winding 29.8 miles to the signed trail-head on the right (south) side of the road. (The road turns to a dirt sur-face at 5.3 miles.) Parking is on the north side of the road.

THE HIKE

From the trailhead, hike up a hillside and through two switchbacks at a quarter-mile. After a gain of 200 feet—the most strenuous section of

the hike—reach a saddle at 0.4 mile. Here, look to your right (north) for a footpath that in a few yards leads to a good viewpoint overlooking the Middle Fork of the Boise River.

At the saddle, the trail turns left (south) and rises another 150 feet to where it levels at 1.0 mile. There, you will find a outcropping nestled high above Sheep Creek—a wonderful perch for photographs. Use caution

Sheep Creek drainage

if you venture out to its edge. After you pass the outcropping, begin a gentle descent to a signed junction at 1.4 miles. Turn right (south), and descend nearly another 100 feet to a large stand of ponderosa pines and a campsite. Just beyond this location is a bridge spanning Sheep Creek and the continuation of the Corral Creek Trail, which climbs to 5,400 feet and descends to FR 113. (See hike 39 to read a description of the trail from FR 113.)

Another option to extend the hike is to continue east at the junction at 1.4 mile. From there, the Sheep Creek trail rises about 100 feet and offers good vistas up and down the drainage. At 2.4 miles is a bridge spanning Sheep Creek. This is a good destination for a longer hike.

Beyond the bridge, the hike is strenuous as the trail's grade is much steeper. There are very few trees in this area due to the 1992 Foothills Fire. The Foothills Fire was a super-hot fire reaching temperatures near 2,000°F and reportedly traveled 18 miles in 10 hours. The fire eventually burned 250,000 acres and, unfortunately, destroyed most of the old-growth ponderosa pines farther up the Sheep Creek drainage. The Sheep Creek trail continues about 10.5 miles beyond the bridge and eventually connects with the Roaring River Trail at an elevation of 5,500 feet.

Sheep Creek near destination

39 CORRAL CREEK

Coordinates

Trailhead
   N 43° 35.412'
   W 115° 42.439'
**Second Ford of
Corral Creek**
   N 43° 36.626'
   W 115° 41.478'

Distance: 3.6 miles out-and-back
Total Elevation Gain: 650 feet
Difficulty: 🚶🚶🚶
Elevation Range: 3,700 to 4,300 feet
Topographic Map: Long Gulch, Twin Springs
Time: 2 hours
Season: April through mid-November
Water Availability: Corral Creek
Cautionary Advice: Expect grazing cattle. FR 113 is not maintained in the winter.
Additional Information: Boise National Forest, Mountain Home Ranger District (208) 587-7961
Pit Latrine: No

CORRAL CREEK

East of Arrowrock Reservoir and south of the Boise River is a seldom-traveled trail with meadows, big ponderosa pines, compelling rock formations, and plenty of solitude. The route begins in ponderosa pine forest paralleling the shrub-lined Corral Creek for just under a mile. It then enters a large meadow covered with green grass and sagebrush and comes to a ford of Corral Creek. East of the ford, backpackers will find a few shaded spots to pitch tents near the year-round flowing creek.

The trail continues another half-mile and requires a second ford of Corral Creek. Here, dense understory makes for a logical turnaround spot. Beyond this point, the trail becomes steep as it makes its way up a narrow, V-shaped drainage to the headwaters of Corral Creek. Another destination, albeit a little more challenging, is to continue beyond the second Corral Creek ford another 0.6 mile. You will ascend about 400 feet to a band of outcroppings that extend up the canyon wall. You are likely to see a few nesting raptors in this area, especially in the spring.

View north from the Cottonwood Creek Trail

The drive along the last 7 miles to the trailhead is nearly as reward-ing as the hike. Once across the Boise River, FR 113 rises over 1,300 feet in Slide Gulch to a high saddle at 4,500 feet, offering spectacular views north into the Boise River drainage and beyond to convoluted mountains. Hike in late May if you're looking for spring wildflowers and mid-October for peak fall colors. Near the trailhead along FR 113, you will find a couple of dispersed campsites along Rattlesnake Creek. If you decide to stay in the area, make sure to hike the nearby Trail Creek. (See hike 40.)

DRIVING DIRECTIONS

From the junction of Warm Springs Avenue and ID 21, drive northeast on ID 21 for 9.3 miles. Cross the Mores Creek Bridge. Make an immedi-ate right (east) onto paved FR 268. Drive a winding 22 miles. (The road turns to a dirt surface at 5.3 miles.) Turn right onto Long Gulch Road (FR 113), which immediately crosses a bridge over the Boise River. Reset your tripmeter. Proceed 6.8 miles to the unsigned trailhead on the left (north). There is plenty of parking on the right side of the road opposite the trailhead.

THE HIKE

From the trailhead, hike into old-growth ponderosa pine forest. The trail parallels Corral Creek and comes to an unsigned junction at 0.1 mile. The trail to the right crosses Corral Creek and continues a half-mile to a signed trailhead for Corral Creek. This route is used primarily by equestrians.

Past the unsigned junction, continue northeast under a canopy of large ponderosa pines. At 0.8 mile, the trail leaves the forest and rises a steep 100 feet. It levels again in a large clearing with green grass and sagebrush. The views looking up and down the broad canyon are very good. Ford Corral Creek at 1.3 miles. Continue through open terrain to a second ford of Corral Creek at 1.8 miles. The wooded setting is your destination.

If you want to extend the hike, the trail continues up the narrow canyon. Although this section of canyon lacks conifer trees due to past forest fires, there are wildflowers (late May and June), cottonwoods, shrubs and outcroppings. The grade is very steep and passes a large collection of outcroppings at 2.4 miles. The views from the trail are very good looking back down to Corral Creek. The trail continues up canyon another couple of miles and levels near an elevation of 5,400 feet. It then descends about 4.0 miles to the Sheep Creek trail.

Looking south above the Cottonwood Creek drainage

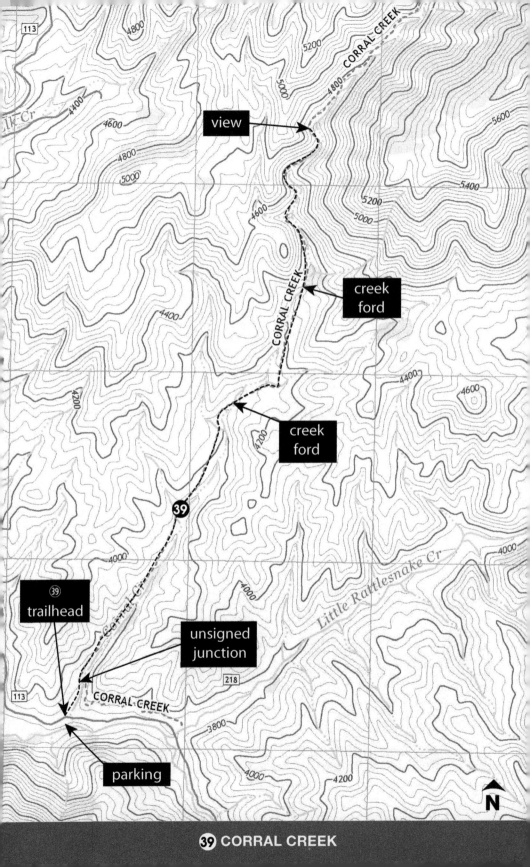

view

creek ford

creek ford

39

trailhead **39**

unsigned junction

113

CORRAL CREEK

218

parking

Little Rattlesnake Cr

N

40 TRAIL CREEK

Distance: 2.5 miles semi-loop
Total Elevation Gain: 350 feet
Difficulty: 👥 👥
Elevation Range: 4,050 feet to 4,400 feet
Topographic Map: Long Gulch, Twin Springs, Arrowrock Reservoir, Grape Mountain
Time: 1.5 hours
Season: April through mid-November
Water Availability: Trail Creek is seasonal. It usually has water in spring and early summer.
Cautionary Advice: A small section of the route (about 400 feet) is not on a trail but is easy to negotiate. FR 113 is not maintained in winter.
Additional Information: Boise National Forest, Mountain Home Ranger District (208) 587-7961
Pit Latrine: No

Coordinates
Trailhead
N 43° 36.689'
W 115° 44.473'
Trail Creek Ford
N 43° 37.282'
W 115° 45.086'

TRAIL CREEK

Few people know much about this surprisingly stunning area south of Arrowrock Reservoir. The hike follows a couple of old primitive forest roads that have been partially retaken by Mother Nature. You will see old-growth ponderosa pines, rolling hills and interesting outcroppings along the journey.

The trail begins with an easy half-mile descent to an unsigned junction. You then veer left, and continue nearly three-quarters of a mile to where the old road disappears. To complete the loop, you will need to hike off-trail about 400 feet through open forest and over tiny Trail Creek to find another old roadbed that takes you back to the unsigned junction.

Trail Creek is seasonal, and there are many excellent locations for a short, remote backpack in late spring. Plus, spring hikers will find several other seasonal streams along the route and many wildflowers. Note: Cattle do graze in the area so there is a chance you will see a few. Hikers looking for additional mileage and scenery can extend the hike by following a footpath to the south side of Arrowrock Reservoir. The drive on FR 113 rises over a 4,500-foot saddle where you will find spectacular vistas north into the Middle Fork of the Boise River drainage.

DRIVING DIRECTIONS

From the junction of Warm Springs Avenue and ID 21, follow ID 21 north for 9.3 miles. Cross the Mores Creek Bridge. Make an immediate right (east) onto the paved FR 268. Drive a winding 22 miles and then turn right onto Long Gulch Road (FR 113), which immediately crosses a bridge over the Boise River. (The road turns to a dirt surface at 5.3 miles.) Reset your tripmeter, and proceed 5.2 miles to FR 221. Turn right on FR 221, and follow this road to a junction at 0.9 mile. Continue along the right fork to the trailhead at 1.0 mile. The first section of FR 221 is rutted (passable with a passenger car) but improves the farther along the road you travel.

THE HIKE

From the parking area, pass through a gated barbed-wire fence and then turn left to the old roadbed. Once on the road, start a gradual descent through open forest. The trail crosses a seasonal creek at 0.3 mile and enters old-growth ponderosa pine forest. Reach an unsigned Y-junction at 0.5 mile.

Turn left (northwest) and then make a gentle descent to another seasonal creek at 0.7 mile. The setting here is beautiful. Many tall trees soar overhead, and there is sufficient level ground to establish a campsite. The route continues northwest as the trees give way to an open clearing, and the roadbed transitions to a singletrack trail. Reenter forest. The trail completely disappears at 1.2 miles where the forest understory becomes dense. Turn right (east) and descend to an easy ford of Trail Creek in 50 yards. Beyond the ford of Trail Creek, there are many fine settings under ponderosa pines for an isolated backpack destination.

Once across Trail Creek, look for another old roadbed in about 75 yards, directly below a beautiful hillside blanketed with outcroppings. If you want to extend the hike, you can turn left and follow the road— eventually transitioning to a singletrack trail—about 2.5 miles with a loss of 800 feet in elevation to the edge of Arrowrock Reservoir. The hike is mostly through open terrain along the sparse valley floor.

To complete the loop hike, turn right and follow the roadbed as it parallels Trail Creek. At 1.6 miles, the roadbed veers right, crosses a culvert and Trail Creek and rises to the unsigned junction where you were earlier. (There are good campsites in this area.) Here, turn left and retrace your steps a half-mile back to the trailhead with an elevation gain of 100 feet.

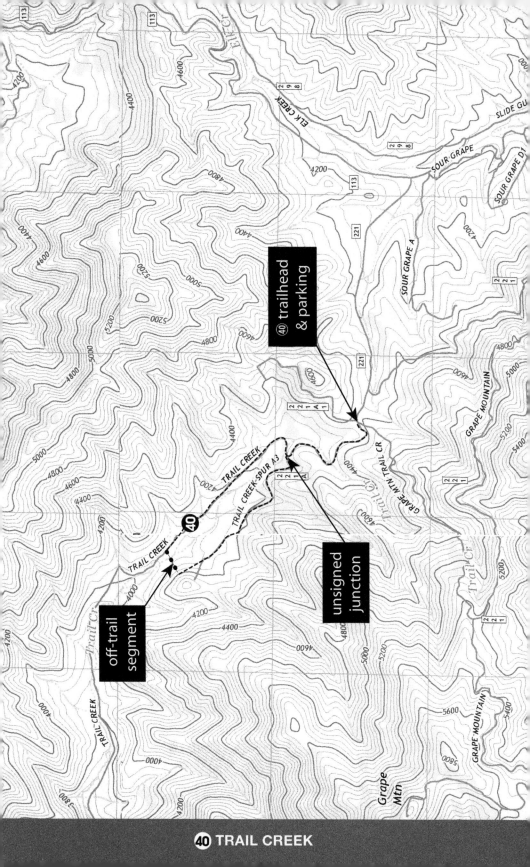

off-trail segment

unsigned junction

㊵ trailhead & parking

㊵ TRAIL CREEK

Distance: 1.0 miles out-and-back (Rattlesnake Spring) 3.4 miles (mini-loop)

Total Elevation Gain: 200 feet (Rattlesnake Spring) 700 feet (mini-loop)

Difficulty: 🚶 or 🚶🚶🚶

Elevation Range: 3,950 to 4,650 feet

Topographic Map: Teapot Dome

Time: 1 hour or 2.5 hours

Season: All year

Water Availability: Rattlesnake Creek

Cautionary Advice: Watch for rattlesnakes during the hot summer months.

Additional Information: Bureau of Land Management, Bruneau Field Office (208) 384-3300

Pit Latrine: No

Coordinates

Trailhead
N 43° 12.398'
W 115° 33.274'

Rattlesnake Springs
N 43° 12.781'
W 115° 33.024'

RATTLESNAKE SPRING

This overlooked user-created trail is certainly off the radar, although it shouldn't be. It is a nice singletrack trail that parallels the willow-lined Rattlesnake Creek through a canyon hemmed by rhyolite cliffs. Although there are no trees, the drainage is scenic, especially in spring when the plant community comes to life.

Before reaching Rattlesnake Spring, there is a level, grassy area that is bisected by the creek. Here, the open hillsides allow for easy off-trail exploration. At a half-mile, the foot trail comes to Rattlesnake Spring where an impressive amount of water flows from a hillside. From the springs, you can ascend a steep 300 feet to the top of a rhyolite ridge that dispenses wonderful vistas of the beautiful, rolling landscape.

Another option is to continue west through the canyon. The foot trail is less obvious along this segment, so you should be comfortable with a little bit of route-finding. The canyon is much narrower than the initial segment of the hike. The drainage is usually dry, but there is an intermittent stream that connects with Rattlesnake Creek in spring. At 1.3

miles, you can complete a mini-loop. A foot trail rises a couple hundred feet above the canyon and provides good vistas of the rugged topography and deep drainage. The trail gets little use, so solitude is almost guaranteed. Cattle do graze in the area, so expect to see some.

Rhyolite outcroppings

DRIVING DIRECTIONS

From I-84 and Broadway Avenue in Boise, follow I-84 east approximately 41 miles to Highway 20 (Exit 95). Turn left on Highway 20, and continue north 7.8 miles to a short, unmarked spur road on the right (north). Drive 0.1 mile to the unsigned trailhead. There is parking for 4 or 5 vehicles.

THE HIKE

From the parking area, pass through a barbed wire gate. (Make sure to close the gate.) From here, follow the singletrack trail as it veers left below rhyolite cliffs. Cross a narrow bridge over Rattlesnake Creek at 0.2

mile. The trail veers left (west) as the canyon opens. Continue alongside the creek. At 0.4 mile, cross a small section of talus and come to Rattlesnake Spring. The surrounding area is quite lush, thanks to the spring, considering its arid environment.

To extend the hike, ford the creek and con-

View southwest from steep ridge above Rattlesnake Spring

173

Bridge over Rattlesnake Creek

tinue west. You will soon see several foot trails. One option is to veer right (north) and then follow one of the foot trails up a nearby steep ridge to its top. The elevation gain is nearly 300 feet. The views are spectacular from the top.

Another option once you ford Rattlesnake Creek is to continue west up the canyon. The canyon narrows and veers north at 0.8 mile. The trail stays along the canyon floor, passing outcroppings at 1.1 miles, and comes to a large rock wall at 1.3 miles. This would be an excellent destination for a 2.6 miles out-and-back hike.

Veer right at the rock wall to complete a mini-loop. (If you look left at the rock wall, you will see a foot path that veers west up the steep hillside. This will be your return for the loop.) At 1.5 miles, the canyon splits. A foot trail leads right (east) but disappears within a quarter-mile below rhyolite cliffs—certainly worthy of a visit.

At the 1.5 mile-canyon split, veer left and continue up the main canyon. The canyon narrows and comes to an unsigned junction at 1.7 miles. Turn left (west), and veer southwest along a prominent, narrow trail cut into the hillside. After a gain of nearly 100 feet, you will emerge on an open plateau with good views down into the canyon. Follow the faint footpath south paralleling the canyon, and at 1.9 miles, begin a 100-foot descent to the canyon floor. Turn right, and retrace your footsteps 1.3 miles back to your vehicle.

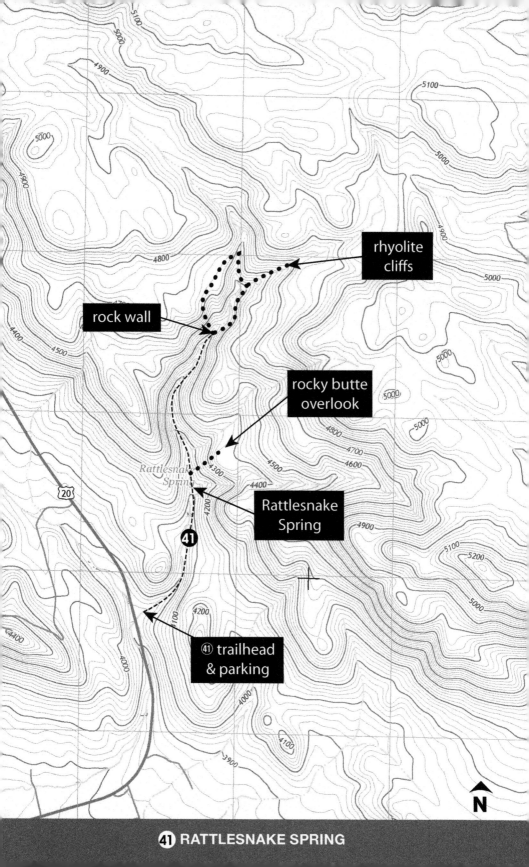

rhyolite cliffs

rock wall

rocky butte overlook

Rattlesnake Spring

Rattlesnake Spring

41

20

41 trailhead & parking

N

42 SWAN FALLS DAM

Coordinates

Trailhead
N 43° 14.088'
W 116° 22.431'
Rocky Knoll
N 43° 12.551'
W 116° 22.895'

Distance: 4.0 miles out-and-back
Total Elevation Gain: 200 feet
Difficulty: 🚶🚶
Elevation Range: 2,300 to 2,450 feet
Topographic Map: Wild Horse Butte
Time: 2 hours
Season: All year
Water Availability: Snake River
Cautionary Advice: Temperatures can soar over 100° F in summer. Watch for rattlesnakes in late spring and summer.
Additional Information: idahopower.com/community-recreation/recreation/
Pit Latrine: Yes

SWAN FALLS DAM

Although not a maintained trail (not much to maintain), this is a wonderful hike that leads upriver from Swan Falls Dam. The first mile follows an old, dirt road south that eventually morphs into a singletrack trail. From here, the canyon narrows, and the trail weaves between basalt boulders that stairstep up the steep, east canyon wall. The route continues as it parallels the Snake River and finally crests a rocky knoll offering exceptional vistas up and down the wide river canyon. This is a perfect place for a picnic.

Although the trail is accessible all year, the optimal time to hike is spring. Starting in mid-March and continuing through June, you are likely to see birds of prey. Although many raptors live in the area year-round, the migrating raptors return during the spring months. Viewing is best in early morning and late evening.

Another advantage to a spring hike is the wildflowers. Look for arrowleaf balsamroot, biscuitroot, blazing stars, buckwheat and other desert wildflowers. The mild bloom starts in April and continues through early June. Winter and fall are also good times to hike. In summer, there are two negatives: slithering rattlesnakes and extreme heat. While in the area, it is a worthy endeavor to tour the Swan Falls Dam.

TRAILHEAD DIRECTIONS

From the Boise Connector (Exit 49), follow I-84 west for approximately 5 miles to Exit 44 for Meridian and Kuna. Turn left on Highway 69, and continue south 7.9 miles to Swan Falls Road. Turn left again, and continue 20.1 miles to a junction near the Swan Falls Dam. Veer left and follow the road past the dam to a large parking area at 20.8 miles. (The road turns to a dirt surface at 20.4 miles.) To find the trailhead, walk another 75 yards beyond the parking area to a locked gate marked with a "No Motor Vehicles" sign. There are a several excellent designated campsites near the trailhead.

THE HIKE

Beyond the locked gate, follow the dirt road as it veers south. Within 500 feet, pass an outcropping just yards off trail that offers good elevated vistas up and down the Snake River. Continue upriver, pass through a fence and arrive at a huge fractured rock at 0.3 mile. The trail then descends 50 feet to where it nearly abuts the Snake River.

The road becomes grassier and narrows as you continue your journey and is relatively level over the next half-mile. At 1.2 miles, the narrow road comes to an unsigned junction marked with a large rock. At the junction, veer right towards the river on a singletrack trail. If you miss this junction, the road meets the singletrack trail in another 400 feet. At 1.3 miles, come to a level, grassy area blanketed with large, basalt boulders set below the encroaching east canyon wall. This setting is an excellent destination for a short hike.

From here, the trail weaves between lichen-covered boulders for a half-mile, 700 feet below charcoal-colored canyon cliffs. At 1.9 miles, begin a 70-foot ascent up a grassy hillside. Crest a saddle at 2.0 miles. At this point, the Snake River is wide and panoramic views are exceptional. At the saddle, there is a rocky knoll to the west (right) that is perched high above the river. This is a great place to take in the views, but it is not recommended for children because there are very steep drop-offs.

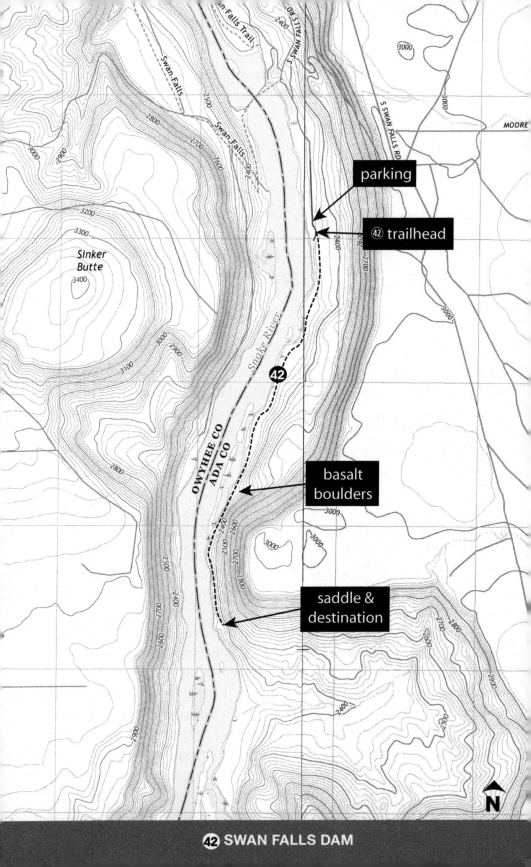

parking

42 trailhead

basalt
boulders

saddle &
destination

Sinker
Butte

Snake River

OWYHEE CO
ADA CO

Swan Falls

Swan Falls

Swan Falls Trail

S SWAN FALLS RD

S SWAN FALLS RD

MOORE

N

42 SWAN FALLS DAM

43 RIVER CANYON TRAIL

Distance: 2.0 miles out-and-back

Total Elevation Gain: 50 feet

Difficulty: 🚶

Elevation Range: 2,300 to 2,350 feet

Topographic Map: Walters Butte, Initial Point

Time: 1 hour

Season: All year

Water Availability: Snake River

Cautionary Advice: Temperatures can soar to more than 100° F in summer. Watch for rattlesnakes during late spring and summer.

Additional Information: Bureau of Land Management, (208) 384-3300

Pit Latrine: Yes, about 100 yards before reaching the trailhead.

Coordinates

Trailhead
N 43° 17.609'
W 116° 25.353'

Y-Junction near Destination
N 43° 17.791'
W 116° 26.483'

RIVER CANYON TRAIL

The River Canyon trail is about 40 miles south of Boise and just a few miles west of Swan Falls Dam. The singletrack trail travels west below canyon cliffs along the edge of the Snake River. The hike description ends at a mile where the canyon widens. There are a few trees nearby with an understory of grass that offer a nice picnic opportunity and easy access to the Snake River.

The trail is within the Morely Nelson Snake River Birds of Prey National Conservation Area. You are likely to see raptors in spring. Hike in early morning or evening for your best opportunities to see hawks, owls, eagles, kestrels and falcons. The best viewing months are mid-March, May and June. Why not April? Most of the raptors are nest-bound as they sit on their eggs.

If you are looking to camp, there are fifteen designated campsites along the way to the trailhead from Swan Falls Dam. Upriver from the dam, you will find five designated campsites and another trail. (See hike 42.) If you would like to extend the hike, you can hike to Halverson Lakes and beyond to Celebration Park.

DRIVING DIRECTIONS

From the Boise Connector (Exit 49), follow I-84 west for approximately 5 miles to Exit 44 for Meridian and Kuna. Turn left on Highway 69. Continue south 7.9 miles to Swan Falls Road. Turn left again, and continue 20.1 miles to a junction near the Swan Falls Dam. Turn right onto Swan Fall Shoreline Road. The road turns to a dirt surface within 500 feet and veers right. The well-graded road ends in 4.3 miles at the trailhead. There are fifteen dispersed camping opportunities along Swan Fall Shoreline Road.

THE HIKE

Snake River near destination

Beyond the gate, follow the wide trail west, paralleling the Snake River. Within 500 feet, come to a rocky knoll extending into the river. To the right of the trail, a small footpath rises 50 feet up a grassy hillside to a couple of flat rocky perches where you can observe the river below. The main trail meanders west along the riverbank and narrows at 0.4 mile.

Soon you pass through an old gate as the scenery improves with the steep basalt cliffs encroaching from the north. The next half-mile is the most scenic with car-sized basalt boulders and large sagebrush abutting the trail. At 0.8 mile, pass through another open gate as the canyon widens. Come to an unsigned Y-junction at 1.0 mile. To find a nice, treed setting to enjoy a break, turn left towards the river, and walk 50 yards to a small stand of trees. Several footpaths continue beyond the trees to the river.

You can extend the hike at the Y-junction. Follow the right fork, and ascend 150 feet over the next half-mile. Continue past a rocky butte south of the trail at just over a mile. From here, you can continue to the two Halverson lakes in about 1.5 miles and on to Celebration Park in another mile. If you have two vehicles, this would be an excellent shuttle hike.

Distance: 2.2 miles out-and-back (first Halverson Lake)
5.0 miles out-and-back (rocky butte)
Total Elevation Gain: 100 feet (first Halverson Lake)
200 feet (rocky butte)
Difficulty: or
Elevation Range: 2,300 to 2,450 feet
Topographic Map: Walters Butte, Initial Point
Time: 1.5 or 2.5 hours
Season: All year
Water Availability: Snake River, Halverson Lakes
Cautionary Advice: Temperatures can easily soar to 100° F in summer. Watch for rattlesnakes during late spring and summer.
Additional Information: Bureau of Land Management (208) 384-3300
Pit Latrine: No. One is available 0.6 mile from the trailhead at Celebration Park.

Coordinates

Trailhead
N 43° 17.492'
W 116° 30.628'
First Halverson Lake
N 43° 17.506'
W 116° 29.656'

HALVERSON LAKES

Stretched along the banks of the Snake River southeast of Celebration Park lie thousands of auburn, gray, and black basalt boulders. The boulders—some over 10 feet in diameter—sprinkled across the desert floor make a striking scene. Geologists estimate that the rocks were deposited here more than 15,000 years ago by the great Bonneville Flood. The boulders are sometimes referred to as melon gravel, a name rumored to have been inspired by a roadside sign labeling the unique rocks "petrified watermelon."

The easy trail to the two Halverson Lakes—the second lake is more like a pond and can dry up by summer—weaves through hundreds of melon gravel boulders along the Snake River Canyon floor. Steep basalt cliffs soar along both sides of the canyon. The first Halverson Lake is reached in about a mile. Cottonwood and aspen trees, willows and other shrubs and melon gravel border the perimeter of the lake. In late October, there is great fall color.

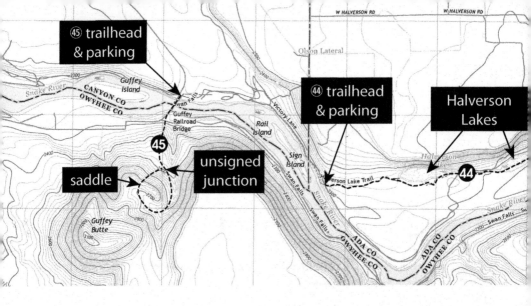

Beyond the first lake, it is an easy walk to the second lake. From the second lake, you can continue more than a mile to a beautiful rocky butte sandwiched between the Snake River and the northern canyon wall. An easy scramble up the south side of the butte takes you about 75 feet above the canyon floor and offers a remarkable perch to observe this unique area.

DRIVING DIRECTIONS

From the Boise Connector (Exit 49), follow I-84 west for approximately 5 miles to Exit 44 for Meridian and Kuna. Turn left on Highway 69. Continue south 7.9 miles to Swan Falls Road. Turn left again, then drive another 11.9 miles. Turn right onto Victory Lane. Follow Victory Lane for 6 miles to the Can-Ada Road. (The road changes from Victory to McDermitt Road and then to Warren Spur.) Cross Can-Ada Road, and continue 1.5 miles to Sinker Road. Turn left and follow the road 2.6 miles to the entrance of Celebration Park. To reach the trialhead, wind through the park for 1 mile to the trailhead. (The road turns to a dirt surface at 0.4 mile.) A high-clearance vehicle is recommended for the last 0.2 mile, but there is a large parking area before the road gets rough.

THE HIKE

En route to the lakes, many user-created spur trails crisscross the area, which can be confusing. Beyond the gated trailhead, walk about 500 feet to a signed junction. Veer left following the sign for the Halverson Lakes Trail. The trail is wide here and veers southeast across a grassy area. At 0.4

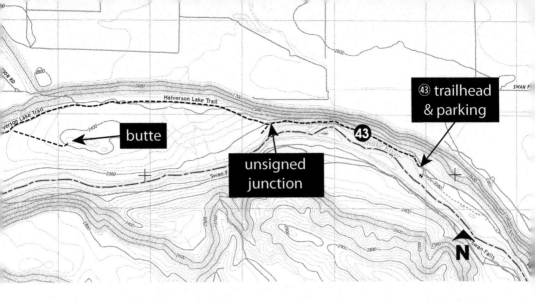

mile, the scenery improves with trailside boulders and large sagebrush. The trail threads the boulders and comes to a junction at 1.0 mile. A foot trail turns left to the west side of the lake.

Continue straight. Within a few feet you will come to an information sign with history about the lakes. At 1.3 miles, you will see the second lake (certainly less interesting), which has little foliage around its perimeter. At 1.5 miles is a junction. The first option is to turn right and then continue another quarter-mile. Turn left at the next junction at 1.7 miles, and go left, which will take you to the base of the butte in about a mile. The other option and about a quarter-mile shorter—albeit with a bit more route-finding—is to continue east at the 1.5 junction. Within a half-mile, a faint footpath veers right (southeast) off the main trail and continues up an incline and then across a level area to the base of the butte. The easiest route to the top of the butte is to approach it from its south side. A faint footpath zigzags to its flat top.

Largest Halverson Lake

45

GUFFEY BUTTE

Coordinates

Trailhead
N 43° 17.975'
W 116° 31.762'

Saddle with View
N 43° 17.457'
W 116° 31.980'

Distance: 1.9 miles
Total Elevation Gain: 500 feet
Difficulty: 🚶🚶
Elevation Range: 2,300 to 2,750 feet
Topographic Map: Walters Butte
Time: 1 hour
Season: All year
Water Availability: None
Cautionary Advice: There is very little shade; it can be extremely hot in summer. Watch for rattle-snakes.
Additional Information: canyonco.org/project/celebration-park/
Pit Latrine: No. One is available at Celebration Park.

GUFFEY BUTTE

This short, semi-loop hike explores the open and rolling landscape directly south of Celebration Park and the Snake River. The primary geological feature is the 3,130-foot Guffey Butte, a flat top mesa with some interestingly shaped volcanic features. The hike enters a wide, basalt-lined canyon and continues west to a saddle. The views from this perch are superb and extend north over 50 miles to the Boise front range. Depending on your off-trail aspirations, there are two ridges you can explore by ascending from the saddle.

From the trailhead, you cross the Snake River on the picturesque Guffey Railroad Bridge. Built in 1897, the 500-foot bridge was an engineering feat in its day and was constructed to help facilitate the transfer of gold and silver ore from Silver City to Nampa. When ore production declined, the railroad was primarily used for passengers and freight. It is named after J.M. Guffey a Pittsburgh capital investor and engineer who helped with the funding and design of its construction.

In the summer of 2015, the 279,000-acre Soda Fire burned in the area. Unfortunately, most of the desert vegetation was burned; very few of the large sagebrush remain. Fall, winter and spring are excellent times to explore the area, but think twice during summer when temperatures soar to triple digits. The trailhead is adjacent to Celebration Park, which has campsites and is Idaho's only archaeological park.

DRIVING DIRECTIONS

There are multiple routes to Celebration Park. Take I-84 west from the Boise Connector (exit 49) approximately 5 miles to exit 44 for Meridian and Kuna. Turn left. Follow Highway 69 for 8.3 miles to Swan Falls Road. Turn left again. Reset your tripmeter. Follow Swan Falls Road 11.9 miles. Turn right onto Victory Lane. Follow Victory Lane for 6.0 miles to a stop sign at Can Ada Road. (The paved road changes from Victory Lane to McDermitt Road and then to Warren Spur.) Cross Can Ada Road and continue 1.5 miles to Sinker Road. Turn left. Follow the road to the Guffey Bridge at 2.6 miles where you can park. The entrance to Celebration Park is on the left.

THE HIKE

About 75 feet after crossing Guffey Bridge, look to your left for a trail that descends through a small gully. It quickly comes to an unsigned junction at a quarter-mile. Here, a trail leads east and parallels the Snake River. Turn right and ascend a steep 100 feet to where the trail levels. If you look straight ahead, you can see the saddle—your destination—sandwiched between two rocky ridges.

Continue south and reach another unsigned junction at 0.6 mile. The trail to the right is very steep and is your return for the semi-loop. (If you want to shorten the hike, take this trail and ascend 250 feet in less than a quarter-mile to the saddle, which is your destination.) Continue south. This route has a more moderate trail grade to reach the saddle. The trail weaves through burned sagebrush and comes to another unsigned junction at 0.9 mile near a large boulder.

Veer right, then ascend along a modest grade up a sandy gully. After a gain of 100 feet in a quarter-mile, enter an area where the terrain is more open. Look to your right (north) for a footpath leading to the top of the saddle. (See map.) The views do not unfold until you reach the saddle, but once there, you see Guffey Bridge, Celebration Park and beyond to the distant Boise Mountains. You can explore the two nearby ridges. Both have interesting volcanic features.

To complete the loop, from the saddle, descend nearly 250 feet to the unsigned junction you bypassed at 0.6 mile. Turn left, and retrace your footsteps back to the trailhead.

46 WILSON CREEK

Coordinates

Trailhead
 N 43° 19.475'
 W 116° 45.188'
End of Canyon
 N 43° 20.124'
 W 116° 44.221'

Distance: 2.8 miles out-and-back
Total Elevation Gain: 300 feet
Difficulty: 🚶🚶
Elevation Range: 3,200 to 3,500 feet
Topographic Map: Wilson Peak
Time: 1.5 hours
Season: All year
Water Availability: Wilson Creek usually flows all year, but it is best to bring your own water.
Cautionary Advice: There is very little shade, and watch for rattlesnakes in summer.
Additional Information: Bureau of Land Management (208) 896-5912
Pit Latrine: No. You will find one at the Wilson Creek Trailhead as you enter the Wilson Creek Travel Management Area.

WILSON CREEK

A few miles southwest of the Snake River and Highway 78, in the foothills of the Owyhee Mountains, is the 28,800-acre Wilson Creek Travel Management Area (WCTMA). Here, you will discover remote canyons, spectacular views of the Snake River Plains and interesting rock formations. The trail system is well-marked with many singletrack routes. Motorized vehicle use is restricted.

Although there are many trails, most are suited for mountain bikers and horse use. There are long stretches without much scenery, and shade is difficult to find. One of the best trails for an easy hike with good scenery is the hike down Wilson Creek. The trail parallels Wilson Creek in a narrow canyon hemmed by beautiful rhyolite rocks and outcroppings. You will need to ford the creek multiple times, but the traverses are nothing more than a rock hop or two. The hike description ends where the canyon widens and scenery becomes less pleasing.

The huge 279,000-acre Soda Fire of 2015 burned in this area. Although there were a few trees and sagebrush in the canyon, many are burned now. However, willows and other flora are starting to grow again along the drainage. Late fall, winter and early spring are all good times to explore the area, but summer temperatures often soar to 100°F. The nearby 5,353-foot Wilson Peak, Wilson Bluff and Wilson Creek are named after an early settler of the area, Marvin Wilson.

DRIVING DIRECTIONS

From downtown Nampa, travel south on 12th Avenue (Highway 45) about 17.5 miles. Turn right (west) on ID 78. Follow ID 78 for 3.1 miles and then turn left on Wilson Creek Road. Reset your tripmeter, and travel 2.5 miles to a Y-junction. Veer right; stay on Wilson Creek Road as the road changes to a dirt surface. Proceed another 3.7 miles to a short spur road (3758) on your right. (You will pass the large Wilson Creek trailhead with an information board and pit latrine at 0.8 mile.) Turn right, and drive 50 yards to the trailhead marked "Trail W100."

THE HIKE

The trail (W100) starts with a short descent to an easy ford of Wilson Creek. Looking west is a very good view of the cliff-faced 4,628-foot Wilson Bluff. The trail then veers northwest, passing an unmarked Y-junction. You can take the right (east) fork at this junction and ford the creek again or continue to a signed junction with W150 at 0.4 mile. Either way, you will need to ford Wilson Creek to continue down the canyon.

From the junction with W150, hike north and enter the narrow canyon holding Wilson Creek. (W150 continues west, gaining 300 feet to a saddle and eventually connects with other trails.) The trail immediately passes a sloped incline with beautiful rhyolite rocks. Here, look for several foot trails that ford Wilson Creek back to its east side. Continue north following the trail down creek. Ford Wilson Creek again at 0.7 mile with many more easy fords over the next half-mile. Along the way, there are many scenic outcroppings and several fine locations to enjoy a secluded picnic.

At 1.4 miles, the canyon widens. This is a good place to turnaround. If you continue another quarter-mile, you will reach the signed junction with trail W140. From this junction, W100 fords the creek again several times and reaches a signed junction with W130 at 1.9 miles. From here, you can stay on W100 to the Wilson Creek trailhead in less than two miles.

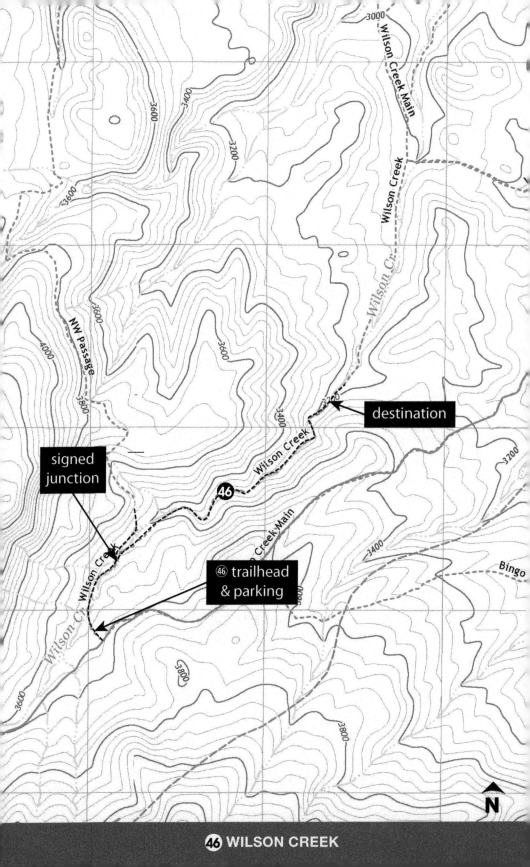

destination

signed
junction

46

trailhead
& parking

Bingo

N

47 JUMP CREEK FALLS

Coordinates

Upper Trailhead
N 43° 28.793'
W 116° 55.498'

Canyon Rim and Rock Outcropping
N 43° 28.608'
W 116° 55.642'

Distance: 0.5 mile out-and-back (Jump Creek Falls)
1.0 miles out-and-back (Canyon Rim and Rock Outcropping)
Total Elevation Gain: 50 feet (Jump Creek Falls)
300 feet (Canyon Rim and Rock Outcropping)
Difficulty: 🚶 or 🚶🚶
Elevation Range: 2,600 to 3,000 feet
Topographic Map: Jump Creek Canyon
Time: 30 minutes to 1 hour
Season: All year
Water Availability: Jump Creek
Cautionary Advice: Watch for poison ivy along the Jump Creek Falls trail.
Additional Information: Bureau of Land Management, Owyhee Field Office (208) 896-5912
Pit Latrine: Yes

JUMP CREEK FALLS

The first thing you notice when planning an outing to Jump Creek Falls is its modest distance. But don't let this truth make you doubt the beauty of this place—a colorful and lush oasis set in the foothills of the Owyhee Mountains. From the lower trailhead, it is a quarter-mile jaunt through a narrow canyon alongside the beautiful Jump Creek. The trail terminates at the end of the canyon where a 60-foot waterfall plummets over a cliff into a shallow pool. Boulders, jungly flora and steep canyon walls complement this ideal setting.

From the upper trailhead, you can walk a very short distance to an overlook of the falls. Or for a longer and more rigorous outing, hike to a beautiful outcropping along the canyon rim. Here, several other user-created trails wander along the rim of the canyon. Due to the steep drop-offs, the canyon rim hike is not recommended for children.

The Jump Creek area can get crowded on weekends, so hike midweek for the possibility of having the place to yourself. Summers can be hot, although the hike to the falls is shielded from the sun most of the day. Also, be aware that poison ivy grows along Jump Creek.

DRIVING DIRECTIONS

At the intersection of ID 55 and U.S. 95 a few miles west of Marsing, go south on U.S. 95 for 2.4 miles. Turn right on Poison Creek Road. Follow Poison Creek Road for 3.2 miles, then turn left on Jump Creek Road. Continue south as the road veers right (west) at 3.6 miles and changes to a dirt surface. At 4.6 miles, enter the Jump Creek Recreation Site. Veer right and reach the upper trailhead at 5.0 miles.

Just before reaching the upper trailhead, the road will split. If you veer left, you can drive another quarter-mile down to the lower trailhead. Sometimes the road to the lower trailhead—mostly in winter—is gated due to unsafe road conditions.

THE HIKE

From the lower trailhead, head south along the wide trail. You soon ford Jump Creek using boulders. Recently, round, flat stepping stones have been placed at the creek ford, which makes the footing much easier. The trail winds past lichen-covered rhyolite boulders and soon reaches the falls. Note: Although user-created foot paths extend above the canyon, avoid these because they are steep, and the footing is unstable. Over the years, there have been many serious injuries, including fatalities.

View north near rock outcropping destination

Jump Creek Falls

To walk to the falls overlook, depart from the upper trailhead. The trail quickly comes to a signed junction for the overlook. Turn left. It is about 300 feet to a lofty perch overlooking the falls.

To hike to the canyon rim and some interesting rock formations, continue west from the overlook junction. The trail rises nearly 300 feet and levels at a quarter-mile. The grade is steep, but there are very good views looking north when you stop to catch your breath. Once the trail levels, continue another 500 feet. Look left for an unsigned junction and a wide trail that leads east. Follow this trail east as it stays on a level grade and reaches a outcropping above the canyon rim at 0.5 mile near an elevation of 3,000 feet. The views into the canyon and beyond to the Snake River Plains are exceptional. Use caution in the area because there are very steep drop-offs. Several foot trails branch in different directions and lead to other outcroppings.

View into canyon from the trailhead

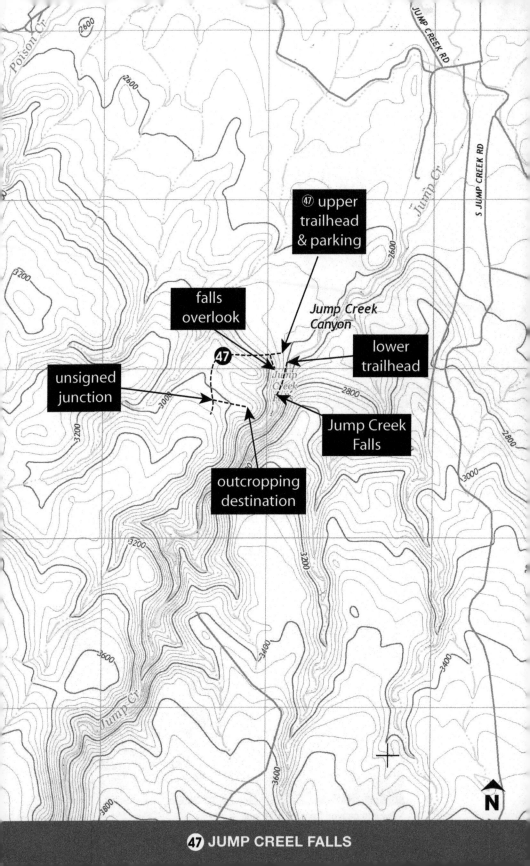

47 JUMP CREEL FALLS

UPPER LESLIE GULCH

Distance: 3.6 miles out-and-back
Total Elevation Gain: 550 feet
Difficulty: 🚶🚶🚶
Elevation Range: 3,750 to 4,300 feet
Topographic Map: Bannock Ridge, Oregon
Time: 2 hours
Season: All year
Water Availability: None
Cautionary Advice: Long pants are recommended because there are several sections where sagebrush encroaches the trail.
Additional Information: Bureau of Land Management, Vale District (541) 473-3144
Pit Latrine: No

Coordinates

Trailhead
N 43° 17.661'
W 117° 15.055'
Destination
N 43° 16.899'
W 117° 13.648'

UPPER LESLIE GULCH

Upper Leslie Gulch canyon leads through a geological wonderland of spectaclar scenery. A 400-foot sheer wall colored in hues of cinnamon and orange looms near the signed trailhead. Within minutes of the start, colorful rock spires, twisting gulches, precipitous cliffs and dramatic rock formations keep hikers guessing what is around the next bend.

The first mile of trail meanders through sagebrush interspersed with dark green juniper trees. After rounding a bend, where the sparse path fades and the canyon opens, the 6,522-foot Mahogany Mountain looms in the far distance. On the left, another canyon with towering cliffs beckons to be explored. The terrain is easily traversed by walking along a dry wash. The canyon eventually tapers where a large juniper tree provides shade under an array of striking rock formations. Adventuresome hikers can experience a slot canyon by hiking another half-mile beyond the juniper tree.

DRIVING DIRECTIONS

At the intersection of ID 55 and U.S. 95, a few miles west of Marsing, turn south onto U.S. 95. Continue 18.9 miles to a sign on the right side of the road ("Leslie Gulch Recreation Area"). Turn right onto McBride Road. Follow this road 8.5 miles to a T-junction, and veer right following the signs for Leslie Gulch. At 10.3 miles, turn left on Leslie Gulch Road. Reset you tripmeter, and continue 9.1 miles to the signed trailhead on the left. There is parking for four or five vehicles.

THE HIKE

From the signed trailhead, hike southeast on the narrow trail. Over the next quarter-mile, there is a lush understory of towering sagebrush, many over 8-feet high. Sandwiching the trail, creme-and-red-colored canyon walls soar 400 feet overhead. At 0.2 mile, veer left as the sagebrush becomes smaller and juniper trees more prolific.

At 0.4 mile, cross a little gully and then continue about 500 feet to an area where there are many juniper trees nestled close to one another. If you look left, you can walk about 75 yards off-trail to a couple of rocky knolls perched about 30 feet up a barren hillside. This is a great mini-destination (1 mile out-and-back) and provides stellar views looking back into the canyon towards the trailhead.

Back on the trail, the route veers right (west) and crosses the gully again. The canyon walls are noticeably farther away. Looking ahead, you will see a beautiful, two-tiered outcropping, and, in the far distance, Mahogany Mountain. At 0.9 mile, the trail comes close to the outcropping. There are many junipers nearby making this another nice stop.

The final segment of the hike continues south. The trail rises about 60 feet up a sagebrush-covered slope and descends through a ravine. It then veers towards a dry wash that drains the canyon and crosses it at 1.1 miles. The remainder of the hike is along the sandy wash, sometimes alongside it if the vegetation is too thick.

At 1.3 miles, look ahead to see a 400-foot colossal rock formation. This is your goal. Over the next-half mile, follow the sandy wash as it meanders up the canyon along a gentle grade. At 1.8 miles, directly below the 400-foot outcropping, a lone, large juniper tree provides a shaded destination. Nearby cliff walls soar overhead, and the setting is quite spectacular.

You can extend the hike by walking east up the wash from the juniper tree. At 2.2 miles, the canyon narrows considerably, and the hiking becomes challenging as you must negotiate large rocks and dense brush. You can proceed about a quarter-mile up to a slot canyon before it becomes too narrow for travel.

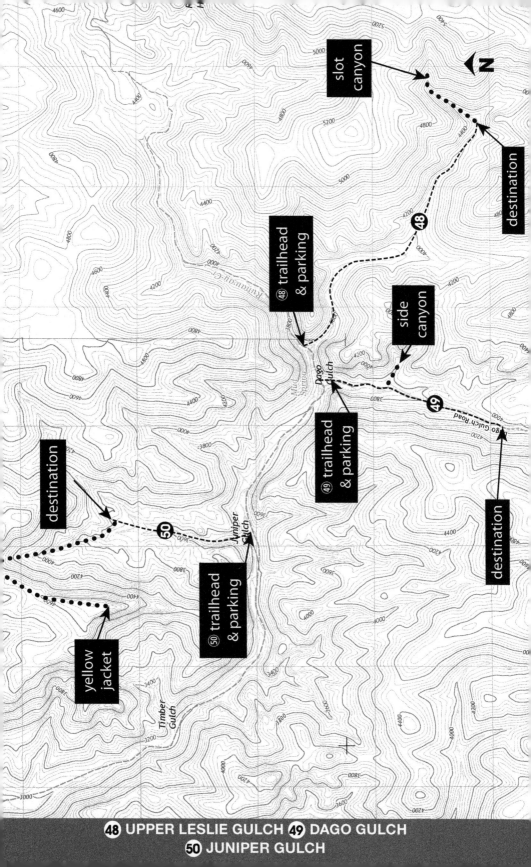

slot canyon

N

destination

48

trailhead & parking

side canyon

49

trailhead & parking

Dago Gulch Road

destination

destination

50

trailhead & parking

Juniper Gulch

yellow jacket

Timber Gulch

Mud Spring

Runaway Cr.

48 UPPER LESLIE GULCH **49** DAGO GULCH
50 JUNIPER GULCH

49 DAGO GULCH

Distance: 1.7 miles out-and-back	

Distance: 1.7 miles out-and-back
Total Elevation Gain: 250 feet
Difficulty: 🚶
Elevation Range: 3,700 to 3,950 feet
Topographic Map: Rooster Comb and Bannock Ridge, Oregon
Time: 1 hour
Season: All year
Water Availability: None
Cautionary Advice: None
Additional Information: Bureau of Land Management, Vale District (541) 473-3144
Pit Latrine: No (There is one about a quarter-mile farther west into Leslie Gulch.)

Coordinates

Trailhead
N 43° 17.465'
W 117° 15.290'

Gate at private property
N 43° 16.786'
W 117° 15.539'

DAGO GULCH

Although the hike up Dago Gulch is along an old dirt road, it is a worthy short hike. The road, closed to motorized users, allows hikers to walk two abreast. Typical of hikes in the Leslie Gulch area, the gulch bisects steep slopes with riveting rock formations and steep cream-and-rust colored cliffs. Although the views are enticing along the way, the best vistas are from the upper reaches of the hike looking back to the sculpted rock formations near the trailhead.

The hike ends at a gate that is the beginning of private property. Here, you can venture off-trail a few yards to a sandy wash where there are junipers, huge boulders and outcroppings perfect for a shaded break. There is a side canyon about a quarter-mile from the trailhead that you can venture a short distance down.

DRIVING DIRECTIONS

At the intersection of ID 55 and U.S. 95, a few miles west of Marsing, turn south onto U.S. 95. Continue 18.9 miles to a sign ("Leslie

View north to the trailhead

Gulch Recreation Area") on the right side of the road. Turn right onto McBride Road. Follow this road 8.5 miles to a T-junction, then veer right. Follow the signs for Leslie Gulch. At 10.3 miles, turn left on Leslie Gulch Road. Reset your tripmeter. Continue 9.3 miles to a road on the left marked with a "Dago Gulch" sign. Proceed 0.2 mile to the signed trailhead. There is parking for four or five vehicles.

THE HIKE

From the gate, walk south on the dirt road. At 0.2 mile, a side canyon branches off to the left (east). A primitive trail leads up this canyon and is a beautiful side diversion for about a quarter-mile. Beyond this point, the route becomes much more challenging.

Back on the road, cross a dry wash immediately past the side canyon. The road's grade steepens and gains 100 feet in elevation to an open hillside at 0.4 mile. Views are exceptional looking back towards Leslie Gulch. Continue south, paralleling the wash. At 0.8 mile, reach the highpoint of the hike, which offers superb vistas. From here, it is only a few yards to a metal gate and private property. This is the end of the hike.

If you are looking for a place to have a secluded picnic, you can descend a few feet into the sandy drainage just before reaching the gate.

Snow-covered foot trail into side canyon

50 JUNIPER GULCH

Coordinates

Trailhead
> N 43° 17.921'
> W 117° 16.227'

Destination
> N 43° 18.559'
> W 117° 16.124'

Distance: 1.8 miles out-and-back
Total Elevation Gain: 350 feet
Difficulty: 🚶 🚶
Elevation Range: 3,450 to 3,800 feet
Topographic Map: Rooster Comb and Bannock Ridge, Oregon
Time: 1 to 1.5 hours
Season: All year
Water Availability: None
Cautionary Advice: None
Additional Information: Bureau of Land Management, Vale District (541) 473-3144
Pit Latrine: Yes

JUNIPER GULCH

Of the hikes described in the Leslie Gulch area, the hike along Juniper Gulch to a wide basin dotted with junipers and beautiful outcroppings is arguably the most scenic. The outing starts with a half-mile jaunt up a dry wash framed with junipers, overhanging rock walls and interesting rock formations. You then ascend an open ridge with superlative views of the multicolored rhyolite and basalt cliffs surrounding the broad basin.

The basin is dotted with hundreds of juniper trees, towering rock formations and sagebrush. The destination of the hike is at the end of the basin under a rocky rampart of interesting outcroppings. The views looking south over the basin are exceptional. To extend the hike, you have several options. You can explore the basin off-trail to find your own secluded haven, or hike up a dry wash along the west side of the basin.

Although not easy, strong hikers can ascend to a high, open saddle above Juniper Gulch and eventually meander to the top of Yellow Jack-

Upper segment of hike in Juniper Gulch

et, a high plateau that divides Timber Gulch and Juniper Gulch. The extensive views from this point are jaw-dropping! Vistas stretch in all directions for as far as the eye can see.

DRIVING DIRECTIONS

At the intersection of ID 55 and U.S. 95 a few miles west of Marsing, turn south onto U.S. 95. Continue 18.9 miles to a sign ("Leslie Gulch Recreation Area") on the right side of the road. Turn right onto McBride Road. Follow this road 8.5 miles to a T-junction. Veer right following the signs for Leslie Gulch. At 10.3 miles, turn left on Leslie Gulch Road. Reset you tripmeter. Continue 10.2 miles to the signed trailhead on your right. There is parking for seven or eight vehicles.

THE HIKE

From the trailhead, the trail veers through sagebrush and turns northeast up a dry wash. Follow the wash as it curves its way up canyon, passing below cliff walls and past beautiful rock formations. At 0.6 mile, the canyon will split. Veer left, and continue about 100 feet to where a large rock blocks the path. You can navigate over the rock. But for outstanding views, turn right up an obvious foot trail that leaves the wash before reaching the large rock.

The foot trail ascends about 50 feet and continues north into the basin. As you ascend, the views of the surrounding terrain are outstanding. Continue along the wide ridge and reach a huge rock formation at 0.8 mile just west of the trail. This is a good area to stop because there are nearby juniper trees for shade. The best spot though is to continue another 400 feet on the obvious path to the base of the cliffs ahead. Look to your left for a towering rock spire. The views looking back down the basin are certainly memorable.

To extend the hike up the canyon, walk back down to the huge rock formation at 0.8 mile and then turn right (west). You will see a couple of faint paths that descend to the dry wash. It doesn't matter which one you take. Once you are in the wash, follow it for about a quarter-mile. The scenery is spectacular. At 0.4 mile (from the huge rock formation), the wash transforms into a grassy and sandy gulch near a few burned junipers. Here you will see a foot path that continues up canyon.

You can continue beyond this point, leaving the junipers behind, and gain a steep 800 feet to the top of a flat plateau. You will find occasional cairns to assist with route finding. Once you reach the plateau, turn left (south), and hike another 0.7 mile with 250 feet of gain to the grassy ridgetop of Yellow Jacket.

View south near 0.8 mile destination

ABOUT THE AUTHOR AND PHOTOGRAPHER

Although Scott Marchant was raised in Central Florida and did not see his first snowfall until he was in college, he has been an avid —some say maniacal—hiker from the first time he saw the Sierra Nevada Mountains. This is his seventh Idaho hiking guidebook, and he spends the majority of his time wandering and happily getting lost in Idaho's beautiful backcountry. Unfortunately, his teenagers no longer like to hike with him because he ventures down too many side trails to see what surprises lurk around the next bend: Any hike with Scott becomes far longer than his hike description. In addition to writing and researching hiking guidebooks, Scott shares Idaho's diverse scenery in an annual wilderness calendar and greeting card line. Although the woods are where Scott prefers to lay his head, his permanent residence is in Boise.

DISCOVER THE
NATURAL BEAUTY OF IDAHO